# 퀵

## 토익
### 실전모의고사

**SET #1**

LC 음원 채점 &
정답 및 해설

지금부터 Actual Test를 진행합니다.
실제 시험과 동일한 방식으로 진행됨을 말씀드리며,
LC 음원은 QR코드로 청취할 수 있습니다.

준비되면 바로 시작하세요!

## LISTENING TEST

In the Listening test, you will be asked to demonstrate how well you understand spoken English. The entire Listening test will last approximately 45 minutes. There are four parts, and directions are given for each part. You must mark your answers on the separate answer sheet. Do not write your answers in your test book.

## PART 1

**Directions:** For each question in this part, you will hear four statements about a picture in your test book. When you hear the statements, you must select the one statement that best describes what you see in the picture. Then find the number of the question on your answer sheet and mark your answer. The statements will not be printed in your test book and will be spoken only one time.

Statment (A), "Some people are paddling through the water," is the best description of the picture, so you should select answer (A) and mark it on your answer sheet.

**1.**

**2.**

*GO ON TO THE NEXT PAGE* ➤

3.

4.

**5.**

**6.**

*GO ON TO THE NEXT PAGE* ➤

## PART 2

**Directions:** You will hear a question or statement and three responses spoken in English. They will not be printed in your test book and will be spoken only one time. Select the best response to the question or statement and mark the letter (A), (B), or (C) on your answer sheet.

7. Mark your answer on your answer sheet.

8. Mark your answer on your answer sheet.

9. Mark your answer on your answer sheet.

10. Mark your answer on your answer sheet.

11. Mark your answer on your answer sheet.

12. Mark your answer on your answer sheet.

13. Mark your answer on your answer sheet.

14. Mark your answer on your answer sheet.

15. Mark your answer on your answer sheet.

16. Mark your answer on your answer sheet.

17. Mark your answer on your answer sheet.

18. Mark your answer on your answer sheet.

19. Mark your answer on your answer sheet.

20. Mark your answer on your answer sheet.

21. Mark your answer on your answer sheet.

22. Mark your answer on your answer sheet.

23. Mark your answer on your answer sheet.

24. Mark your answer on your answer sheet.

25. Mark your answer on your answer sheet.

26. Mark your answer on your answer sheet.

27. Mark your answer on your answer sheet.

28. Mark your answer on your answer sheet.

29. Mark your answer on your answer sheet.

30. Mark your answer on your answer sheet.

31. Mark your answer on your answer sheet.

## PART 3

**Directions:** You will hear some conversations between two or more people. You will be asked to answer three questions about what the speakers say in each conversation. Select the best response to each question and mark the letter (A), (B), (C), or (D) on your answer sheet. The conversations will not be printed in your test book and will be spoken only one time.

32. What are the speakers discussing?
    (A) The delivery department
    (B) Each other's text messages
    (C) The advertising plan
    (D) Cooker line

33. What caused the delay?
    (A) Using the delivery system
    (B) Making improvements
    (C) Beginning the advertisement in advance
    (D) Putting the handles in place

34. What does the man say he is waiting for?
    (A) A cooker
    (B) Replacement parts
    (C) The fans
    (D) A marketing project

35. What kind of company will the speakers most likely work for?
    (A) An energy company
    (B) A building maintenance company
    (C) A power station
    (D) A construction company

36. What concern does the woman have?
    (A) Whether they can keep the construction cost in the budget.
    (B) Whether they can make insulation panels
    (C) Whether they can include energy saving features
    (D) Whether they can install insulation panels properly

37. What does the man say he will do?
    (A) Design an office building.
    (B) Request Mr. Kurt for some help.
    (C) Check who discussed the McDonald's company.
    (D) Begin to include insulation panels in the design.

38. What are the speakers discussing?
    (A) Consumer complaints
    (B) Reviews of the old model
    (C) Product design
    (D) New idea for the items

39. According to the woman, why were changes made?
    (A) To satisfy the customer's needs
    (B) To respond to customer feedback
    (C) To use the simplified design
    (D) To make eco-friendly products

40. What does the man inquire about?
    (A) The launching date
    (B) The address of the markets
    (C) The production process
    (D) The discount rate

41. Why is the man calling the woman?
    (A) To place his sign in his store
    (B) To introduce his wife to Ms. Hazzel
    (C) To announce the Goldstein Mall Association
    (D) To inform a local regulation

42. What does the woman say she will do?
    (A) She will call the Goldstein Mall Association.
    (B) She will take notes about the advertisement.
    (C) She will remove the sign board immediately.
    (D) She will recognize the regional rules.

43. What does the man recommend the woman to do?
    (A) To post her goods on the web site
    (B) To advertise in a local magazine
    (C) To read the business articles
    (D) To receive the support from his neighbor

*GO ON TO THE NEXT PAGE*

44. What are the speakers discussing?

(A) The registration process
(B) The attachment file
(C) The e-mail's number
(D) The bike race

45. What is the purpose of the telephone call?

(A) To register for the participant number
(B) To get her shirt from the city
(C) To confirm whether her name is on the registration list
(D) To find the mailing system

46. What does the man ask the woman to bring to the information booth?

(A) Her participant list
(B) Her registration date
(C) Her ID card
(D) Her mobile phone number

___

47. Why was the woman surprised?

(A) The new company's business.
(B) The man's retiring
(C) Her new position in this cosmetic company
(D) A brilliant advertising team

48. What does the man say about this cosmetic company?

(A) Its successor is not interested in the new company's business.
(B) It will do well in leading the chemical industry.
(C) It will have many job offers.
(D) It has an excellent advertising department.

49. Why does the woman ask for more time?

(A) To think over the company's job offer
(B) To tell the president in advance
(C) To appreciate her operation
(D) To form a marketing team

50. What are the speakers discussing?

(A) A summer event
(B) A parking lot
(C) A renovation of Severs Park
(D) A business location

51. What does the man think about Severs Park area?

(A) It has a small floating population.
(B) Its rent is lower than he expected.
(C) Its transportation is convenient.
(D) It already has many shopping malls.

52. What do the women want to do?

(A) They want to open a new shop in Severs Park.
(B) They want to transfer their office to a new location.
(C) They want to increase the rent.
(D) They want to drive their car to summer beach.

___

53. Why is the man calling?

(A) To receive feedback from his clients
(B) To reschedule an appointment
(C) To join the club
(D) To get an order

54. What does the woman mean when she says, "I wish I could"?

(A) She won't check her calendar mow.
(B) She wishes that he cancels his next engagement.
(C) She wants him to come to her office.
(D) She can't meet him at 12:00.

55. What will the woman do next?

(A) Call a cafe
(B) Go for a drive
(C) Postpone her appointment
(D) Send her documents to Lorenzo Hollaway

**56.** What will Ms. Roland's job most likely be?

(A) A vendor
(B) A owner of shopping mall
(C) A landlord
(D) A constructor

**57.** Why does Ms. Roland deny Mr. Fraiser's offer?

(A) Because she is too busy
(B) Because she is out of town
(C) Because she is discussing Mr. Norris
(D) Because she is in Dupont shopping mall

**58.** Where will Mr. Norris meet Mr. Fraiser?

(A) In Mr. Norris' house
(B) In Mr. Fraiser's office
(C) On Pinetree street
(D) On Dupont shopping mall

---

**59.** Where will the speakers most likely be?

(A) At a hotel
(B) At a studio
(C) At a shopping mall
(D) At a hospital

**60.** What does the woman mean when she say, "That's strange"?

(A) The schedule has changed.
(B) An employee is in the office.
(C) She was surprised that a device was out of order.
(D) She put some equipment in a wrong place.

**61.** What does the woman suggest to do?

(A) To use someone's phone
(B) To record a presentation
(C) To replace the battery with a new one
(D) To check the chargeable level

## PROGRAM

| Performer | Time |
|---|---|
| Elder | 19:00 ~ 19:30 |
| Hartley | 19:30 ~ 20:00 |
| Gilbert | 20:00 ~ 20:30 |
| Milton | 20:30 ~ 21:00 |

**62.** Why did the program change?

(A) Because Hartley plays two pieces.
(B) Because Elder takes too long.
(C) Because Milton can't play in his turn.
(D) Because Hartley starts a little late.

**63.** Look at the graphic. Who will perform last?

(A) Elder
(B) Hartley
(C) Gilbert
(D) Milton

**64.** What kind of performance will Mr. Milton do?

(A) Music
(B) Dancing
(C) Drama
(D) Opera

GO ON TO THE NEXT PAGE

| OFFICE EXTENSIONS | |
| --- | --- |
| Boardroom | ext. 035 |
| Marketing | ext. 028 |
| General | ext. 049 |
| Accounting | ext. 030 |

## SHIPPING FARE

| AMOUNT | FARE |
| --- | --- |
| 1,000 | $199.00 |
| 2,000 | $99.00 |
| 3,000 | $00.00 |
| 10,000 | $00.00 |

65. Why is the woman calling?

(A) To pick up her mobile phone message
(B) To find directions to the building
(C) To contact an employee at this office
(D) To ask the receptionist

66. What is the woman looking at now?

(A) The directory
(B) Her mobile phone
(C) The floor guide map
(D) The reception desk

67. Look at the graphic. Which extension number will the woman dial?

(A) Ext. 028
(B) Ext. 030
(C) Ext. 035
(D) Ext. 049

68. What does the man ask the woman to do?

(A) To compromise with the shipping fare
(B) To order less supplies than last time
(C) To consult with delivery department
(D) To check the inventory

69. What does the woman indicate about the shipping price?

(A) The manufacturer will review the inventory.
(B) The supplier has no items in his warehouse.
(C) Another supplier will offer a good proposal.
(D) A larger order will reduce the shipping cost.

70. Look at the graphic. How many steel cases will the woman order?

(A) 1,000
(B) 2,000
(C) 3,000
(D) 10,000

## PART 4

**Directions:** You will hear some talks given by a single speaker. You will be asked to answer three questions about what the speakers say in each talk. Select the best response to each question and mark the letter (A), (B), (C), or (D) on your answer sheet. The talks will not be printed in your test book and will be spoken only one time.

71. What does the speaker inform listeners of?
    (A) The location of Jeremy hall
    (B) The proximity to South hall
    (C) The distance from Jeremy hall to South hall
    (D) The renovation of the parking area next month

72. What will be available to staff?
    (A) A reimbursement of the transportation fees
    (B) A subway pass
    (C) A complimentary shuttle service
    (D) A request of parking fees

73. What will employees be required to do?
    (A) They must check the company website.
    (B) They must present their ID card to the driver.
    (C) They must ask the company to park outside South hall.
    (D) They must pay their fare to the driver.

74. Why does the speaker apologize?
    (A) Because he postponed the conference
    (B) Because he met the marketing director today
    (C) Because he had a different arrangement
    (D) Because he turned off the light

75. What are the listeners asked to do?
    (A) To express their appreciation
    (B) To compensate for the fund
    (C) To meet attendees' need
    (D) To give honest feedback for the newspaper

76. What will the listeners receive later today?
    (A) A gift
    (B) A ticket
    (C) A reward
    (D) An item

77. What most likely is the speaker's job?
    (A) A programmer
    (B) A florist
    (C) A reporter
    (D) A gardener

78. What will be discussed today?
    (A) The upcoming annual flower show
    (B) The program of Southworth radio
    (C) The gardening tips
    (D) The shared tricks

79. According to the speaker, what can the listeners do on the Southworth radio's website?
    (A) They can watch the Southworth radio's website
    (B) They can prepare for the flower show.
    (C) They can exchange free tickets for cash.
    (D) They can complete the application form.

80. According to the speaker, what happened at the library recently?
    (A) A remodeling
    (B) A welcoming party
    (C) A yearly meeting
    (D) A construction of a wing

81. What is the purpose of the meeting?
    (A) To include the quarterly volunteer
    (B) To welcome the opening of a library
    (C) To construct a new wing
    (D) To assign volunteer work

82. What are the listeners asked to do?
    (A) To complete the schedule
    (B) To send the updated time
    (C) To indicate availability
    (D) To keep a book collection

*GO ON TO THE NEXT PAGE*

83. What type of business is being advertised?

(A) Editing a voice
(B) Customizing a logo
(C) Marketing a brand
(D) Analyzing the business information

84. What does the business specialize in?

(A) Encoding the visual files
(B) Packaging design
(C) Serving customers
(D) Wrapping the products

85. Why should listeners visit the company's web-site?

(A) To view our portfolio or recent work
(B) To guarantee the market share
(C) To check the recent trend
(D) To take part in sales conference

86. Who is the announcement intended for?

(A) Conference participants
(B) Doctors using medical technology
(C) Technicians
(D) Keynote speakers

87. What will the listeners do today?

(A) They will hold a meeting.
(B) They will give their speech.
(C) They will be the speakers.
(D) They will select from many relevant conferences.

88. What is said about Dr. Dryden?

(A) He will put off his address.
(B) He will notify the program of his fellow.
(C) He will give medical technology to a speaker.
(D) He will share his idea with a worker.

89. Who is the advertisement intended for?

(A) People who are dismissed at Muscle Brother Gym
(B) People who can't train too hard
(C) People who will receive the waist surgeries
(D) People who want to walk in the gym

90. What does the man mean when he says, "Here's how it works"?

(A) He will exercise at Muscle Brother Gym.
(B) He will demonstrate a product's recommended usage.
(C) He will run too hard.
(D) He will manage the low-impact program.

91. According to the speaker, what is true about this advertisement?

(A) He experienced weight loss.
(B) He contacted the manufacturer of a running machine.
(C) He called off his training program.
(D) He signed up for his surgery.

92. What is the announcement mainly about?

(A) Target shopping mall
(B) Cordova High School
(C) Miami beach
(D) A fundraising event

93. What are the listeners asked to do?

(A) To wash the parking lot signs
(B) To take their cars to the event
(C) To host a customer's meeting
(D) To donate their funds to Tracy

94. What does the woman mean she says, "Why not help us"?

(A) Everyone can do it.
(B) They need to help us.
(C) Only you can do it.
(D) They may do it by themselves.

## Footgear Sale

| Thu. | Kids' & Women's |
|------|-----------------|
| Fri. | Men's |
| Sat. | All shoes |
| Sun. | Back to normal |

**95.** What is limited about this sale?

(A) What kind of shoes that were selected

(B) What kind of colors the shoes come in

(C) How many pairs get the discount

(D) What kinds of designs were left

**96.** How much is the discount?

(A) 20%

(B) 25%

(C) 33%

(D) 50%

**97.** Look at the graphic. Which day will have a change?

(A) Thursday

(B) Friday

(C) Saturday

(D) Sunday

## SCHEDULE

| Time | Program |
|------|---------|
| 6:00 P.M. | Keynote Speech |
| 6:30 P.M. | Panel Discussion |
| 7:00 P.M. | Closing Remarks |
| 7:30 P.M. | Reception |

**98.** Where will the speaker probably be?

(A) At a volunteer meeting

(B) At an evening music festival

(C) At an award ceremony

(D) At a mobile phone demonstration

**99.** What are the listeners asked to do?

(A) To cater for a company reception

(B) To turn off or silence their mobile phones

(C) To reschedule this evening's arrangement

(D) To thank local government officers

**100.** Look at the graphic. When will the reception start?

(A) At about 6:30 P.M.

(B) At about 7:00 P.M.

(C) At about 7:30 P.M.

(D) At about 8:00 P.M.

**This is the end of the Listening test. Turn to Part 5 in your text book.**

*GO ON TO THE NEXT PAGE*

# READING TEST

In the Reading test, you will read a variety of texts and answer several different types of reading comprehension questions. The entire Reading test will last 75 minutes. There are three parts, and directions are given for each part. You are encouraged to answer as many questions as possible within the time allowed.

You must mark your answers on the separate answer sheet. Do not write your answers in your test book.

## PART 5

**Directions:** A word or phrase is missing in each of the sentences below. Four answer choices are given below each sentence. Select the best answer to complete the sentence. Then mark the letter (A), (B), (C), or (D) on your answer sheet.

101. Section directors are required to help their subordinates with their assignments ------- they have to meet a tight deadline.

(A) if
(B) because
(C) when
(D) though

102. A recent inter-company's survey reports that ------- 50 % of clients are dissatisfied with the quality of service they have in local shops.

(A) nearly
(B) more
(C) less
(D) fewer

103. ------- the vehicle was under the warranty, GM agreed to replace the defective part with a new one at no cost.

(A) In order that
(B) So that
(C) Now that
(D) Although

104. If you have a special meal -------, why not ask our friendly staff, and we will do our best to accommodate your needs.

(A) concept
(B) menu
(C) request
(D) idea

105. Negotiations to relocate the restaurant to the downtown area is underway, ------- the difficulty caused by the lack of parking space.

(A) amid
(B) among
(C) across
(D) between

106. It is very dangerous to operate the machine ------- a technician's assistance in such a construction site.

(A) without
(B) through
(C) including
(D) with

107. Whether the executives will step down or not is the most important issue ------- this afternoon.

(A) to discuss
(B) to have discussed
(C) to be discussed
(D) to have been discussed

108. Because Ms. Courtney Brown's first book about a ------- life was widely recognized and became sold out, Mr. Kevin Tyler's second edition will be revealed soon.

(A) success
(B) successful
(C) successfully
(D) succeed

109. As of ------- week, at least one form of identification will be necessary when a client wants a new membership card to be issued.
   (A) near
   (B) recent
   (C) close
   (D) next

110. The new security system enables us to protect our facilities as ------- as possible.
   (A) efficient
   (B) efficiently
   (C) efficiency
   (D) most efficient

111. Hitel-Com can save you up to 50 percent on international phone calls, while giving you maximum clarity and -------.
   (A) dependability
   (B) depend
   (C) dependable
   (D) dependably

112. Tour de Monde Magazine's revised edition for tourists has caused some apprehension ------- the readers due to some misleading information.
   (A) only
   (B) how
   (C) between
   (D) among

113. In an effort to reduce expenses, we are looking ------- a creative way to enhance worker productivity.
   (A) at
   (B) for
   (C) into
   (D) on

114. Local Business Monthly, a magazine intended for the general public, contains a wealth of descriptive ------- so that everyone can interpret the difficult subjects more easily.
   (A) pictures
   (B) graphs
   (C) bulletins
   (D) tables

115. Because of an unexpected high demand for organic goods, we must quickly ------- production.
   (A) expand
   (B) decrease
   (C) permit
   (D) forbid

116. Ms. Monica Spears, the president of Marconini Electronics, said the new 4G mobile phone is so ------- that the company is struggling to meet demand.
   (A) fashionable
   (B) popular
   (C) common
   (D) general

117. IF NATURE is the name of our competitor, located in Australia, always has the advantage of ------- with the cosmetic market.
   (A) focus
   (B) observance
   (C) compliance
   (D) familiarity

118. To reduce expenses, Ms. Lisa, who is in charge of shipping, has decided that we should ------- the original container into another one.
   (A) transfer
   (B) confer
   (C) infer
   (D) refer

119. Common people were not even allowed to own gold, but it may ------- by a powerful person.
   (A) own
   (B) be owning
   (C) have owned
   (D) have been owned

120. Global leaders have responded quite differently to yesterday's announcement from France declaring that they will veto a NATO ------- to support an America-led Iran war.
   (A) resolve
   (B) resolved
   (C) resolving
   (D) resolution

GO ON TO THE NEXT PAGE

121. A common mistake made by owners is purchasing expensive hardware without knowing how to use it, and -------, employees are hired to operate certain kinds of business software.

(A) by the way
(B) as a result
(C) in addition
(D) in fact

122. The configuration of the YNG-77 laptop is very stable but the design of its keyboard is -------.

(A) comfort
(B) ideal
(C) intensive
(D) inconvenient

123. Phillips Co. is a ------- company in the electronic industry, due to its high quality items and superior customer service.

(A) lead
(B) leads
(C) leading
(D) led

124. The diagnostic process must carefully explore many of ------- problems, not only to provide appropriate diagnoses, but also to identify early signs or risk factors.

(A) this
(B) these
(C) whose
(D) another

125. Korea's civil law ------- all employees to up to 12 weeks off to attend to serious health conditions which they or their immediate family members may have.

(A) enables
(B) entrusts
(C) entitles
(D) enlarges

126. Tuition fees are $50,000, ------- course books and a daily meal plan, but exclusive of other materials and living expenses.

(A) eligible for
(B) responsive to
(C) dependent on
(D) inclusive of

127. The age requirements for hiring flight attendants vary slightly to ------- from different companies.

(A) and
(B) if
(C) which
(D) therefore

128. Ms. Freemont, the chairperson of the planning committee, prefers that directors attend ------- the conference in July or the workshop in August.

(A) whether
(B) either
(C) which
(D) neither

129. Each year, Dupont Co. ------- some money to the starving children around the world.

(A) provides
(B) donates
(C) allocates
(D) promotes

130. With providers launching new deals with competitive rates on a regular -------, there are plenty of products to choose from.

(A) way
(B) basis
(C) period
(D) cause

## PART 6

**Directions:** Read the texts that follow. A word, phrase, or sentence is missing in parts of each text. Four answer choices for each question are given below the text. Select the best answer to complete the text. Then mark the letter (A), (B), (C), or (D) on your answer sheet.

**Questions 131-134** refer to the following article.

---

**CONSERVATION PROGRAM for ECO-HUMANE by National Zoo**

-------. ECO-HUMANE, the conservation branch of the Zoo, works around the world to
**131.**
conserve animal species and the habitats in which they live. -------, over the past several
**132.**
years, the ECO-HUMANE program has supported conservationists in their efforts to

maintain Surabaya Zoo, Jawa Timur, Indonesia.

In May, ECO-HUMANE staff went to Jawa Timur to conduct a conservation assessment.

The findings of the trip led to the zoo to organize a humanitarian aid campaign to benefit

those people living around Surabaya. Through December 31, we are collecting donations

of clothing and equipment to send to the people of Surabaya and to conservation

organizations ------- to the care of Surabaya's wildlife. ------- more information or to donate
**133.**                                          **134.**
cloths, tools, camping equipment or to make a cash donation, please call (031) 567-

4708.

---

131. (A) The National Zoo takes an important role to announce conservation programs abroad
    (B) The National Zoo works to increase animal species and the habitats in which they live
    (C) The National Zoo plays an active role in conservation programs nationally and internationally
    (D) The National Zoo helps conservationists to expand Surabaya Zoo, in Jawa Timur, Indonesia

132. (A) In addition
    (B) In general
    (C) By the way
    (D) For example

133. (A) related
    (B) dedicated
    (C) aggravated
    (D) transferred

134. (A) In
    (B) On
    (C) About
    (D) For

GO ON TO THE NEXT PAGE

**Questions 135-138** refer to the following advertisement.

Welcome !

Thailand travels is a tour and trekking company based in Bangkok. We have been providing high quality tours and trekking for visitors to Bangkok since 2020. We specialize in organizing tours and treks for private groups, providing either standard or customized itineraries. Our standard itineraries take you to see and experience – temples, handicraft centers, elephant camps, traditional native villages, bamboo rafting, fantastic scenery and much more. Our customized itineraries will take you ------- you would like to go in Bangkok.
                                                                                    **135.**

If you book a tour or trek with us, you will travel in your own private air conditioned vehicle, with your own guide and driver. Our goal is to give service that provides people with more than the normal package tour. -------.
                                            **136.**

We make it possible for our clients to ------- enjoy their time with us but also learn more
                                                    **137.**
about Bangkok and its culture. We are continually looking for places to add to our itineraries that focus on different aspects of Thai culture. With our wide variety of programs ------- , there is something for everyone. Book your adventure today through our website.
**138.**

135. (A) whatever
     (B) whenever
     (C) wherever
     (D) however

136 (A) The tours are for package ones, so once you book a trip you shouldn't cancel it
     (B) Unless you book a tour, you won't be given your own private air-conditioned vehicle
     (C) The tours are for private groups, so once reserved, departure and itinerary are guaranteed
     (D) The places will focus on different aspects of Bangkok's culture

137. (A) not
     (B) neither
     (C) both
     (D) not only

138. (A) visible
     (B) considerable
     (C) imaginable
     (D) available

**Questions 139-142** refer to the following memo.

To : Ms. Heather Tyler

From : Mr. Wilson Bradley

Sub : Letter of appreciation

Dear Ms. Heather Tyler

Thank you for your kind letter regarding your ------- treatment by one of our employees. A
                                            **139.**
copy of your letter has been forwarded to the personnel department and will be included in

the employee's file.

It is rare that a customer takes the time to write a letter of appreciation. I felt moved to

reward your ------- .
           **140.**

Please accept the enclosed certificate, which, when presented, will entitle the bearer to a

ten percent discount on the merchandise being purchased at that time.

This is a small token of our appreciation to customers ------- yourself. Without people
                                                 **141.**
like you, we wouldn't have been able to grow and prosper in this highly competitive

marketplace.

-------.
**142.**

Wilson Bradley

---

**139.** (A) except
    (B) exception
    (C) exceptional
    (D) exceptionally

**140.** (A) initiative
    (B) advantage
    (C) bluntness
    (D) effort

**141.** (A) insomuch as
    (B) such as
    (C) same as
    (D) so as

**142.** (A) As a member of our company, I
       will accept your treatment of our
       employee
    (B) We will enable you to raise market
       share in this field
    (C) It is important to satisfy our
       customers in this highly competitive
       marketplace
    (D) Again, on behalf of our entire
       organization, I sincerely thank you
       for your kindness

GO ON TO THE NEXT PAGE ➤

**Questions 143-146** refer to the following e-mail.

---

TO: Stanford Alumni <stanfordalumni@stanfordaeb.org>
FROM: Leon Buffer <leonno1@stanfordaeb.org>
Date : May 1
Subject: Stanford Alumni Employment Bulletin - Advertisement for President

I found the wording of your advertisement with emphasis on leadership, innovation, and change quite intriguing. ------- is my resume in response to your advertisement.
143.

Most recently, I became the President of Wendy Coop, which was in bad shape, but my contribution lead the company to the best ------- in its history. Previously I worked
144.
successfully in a variety of unusual situations, including the startup of a significant division of Goodman and the turnaround of Atlantic Biochemical.

In each of these situations, the problems or opportunities differed widely. ------- they all
145.
demanded the ability to size up the situation, assess the reasonable alternatives, and execute a plan of action. My track record shows that I am able to do this.

With regard to the requirement for manufacturing experience, I have worked 10 years in mining and milling operations, where I gained great insight in the matter of production problems. Additionally, I was the President of Wendy Coop with full responsibility for all operations and financial activities. I am free to travel and open to relocation. -------.
146.

Thank you for your interest.

---

143. (A) Attach
    (B) Attaching
    (C) Attached
    (D) Attachment

144. (A) potentiality
    (B) capability
    (C) performance
    (D) liability

145. (A) However
    (B) Moreover
    (C) Therefore
    (D) Generally

146. (A) I would like to travel abroad anytime and to gained great insight in the matter of production problems
    (B) I was in charge of all operations and financial activities on Wendy 10 years ago
    (C) My career shows that I am able to work in mining and milling operations
    (D) I would welcome the opportunity to meet you and further discuss your requirements

**Directions:** In this part you will read a selection of texts, such as magazine and newspaper articles, e-mails, and instant messages. Each text or set of texts is followed by several questions. Select the best answer for each question and mark the letter (A), (B), (C), or (D) on your answer sheet.

**Questions 147-148** refer to the following announcement.

---

*The Lawrence Festival of Edinburgh*

Free Chance
Open-air performance in Edinburgh Park

"Lady Chatterley's Lover"

March 3rd-17th : Nightly except Sundays.
March 16th    : 1:00 p.m. matinee, no evening performance.

Monday performances will be signed for the hearing impaired
Refreshments will be served to the hearing impaired at no cost.

Valuable life-related lectures by famous scholars start at 5:00 p.m.;
Performances start at 7:00 p.m.

(331) 534-8356 or www.edinburghfestival.com

---

147. When does the open-air performance end?

    (A) March 2nd
    (B) March 10th
    (C) March 15th
    (D) March 17th

148. Whom will the Monday performances be prepared for?

    (A) People with a hearing problem
    (B) People with a good listening ability
    (C) People with a negative attitude towards life
    (D) People with a mental problem

GO ON TO THE NEXT PAGE

**Questions 149-150** refer to the following text message chain.

| | |
|---|---|
| **Text Message** | _ □ × |

**Todd Mir**
10:08

Shawn, I'm supposed to present the advertisement for the Red Hot Vacation people on Friday at 2:00 P.M., but can you cover for me?

**Shawn Green**
10:09

Why not? What's up? You usually pitch the ideas to the client.

**Todd Mir**
10:11

Mandy Chemicals called. My Friday meeting with them has to be at 2:30 P.M., not 11:30 A,M.

**Shawn Green**
10:13

I understand. I'll let you know how the Red Hot Vacation people react.

**Todd Mir**
10:15

Please do. Howard Nelson at Red Hot Vacation is never shy about providing feedback.

**Shawn Green**
10:17

He's way better than Karen Mandy. She never reacts during presentations but has a half dozen complaints the next day.

| Send |
|---|

149. What company does Todd Mir and Shawn Green most likely work for?

(A) An advertising company
(B) A chemical company
(C) A resort
(D) A hotel

150. At 10:15 A.M., what does Todd Mir mean when he says, "Please do"?

(A) He wishes the customer will be less influenced.
(B) He is interested in the client's positive reaction.
(C) He wants the client to send feedback to him.
(D) He is approving Mr. Green's offer.

From: Tom Crown
To: Utah Yamaguchi
Date: May 12, 2024
Subject: Decline to interview referred job applicant

Dear Mr. Yamaguchi,

Since I have been away from the office for a few days, I didn't get a chance to read your e-mail until today.

While I am sure the young man you recommended is great, in my opinion he doesn't deserve the position unless he is truly exceptional and perfect for it. I also believe it wouldn't be fair to our employees to interview him at this time.

We currently have to dismiss thirty two employees, and there is no way that I could justify hiring someone new under these circumstances. We hope that in time, our business will be able to hire new employees, but now is not the right time.

I am sorry to disappoint you. As you know, under the right circumstances, we would always be looking for young and smart people with potential. But this is not the appropriate time to hire new employees.

Thank you for understanding.

Yours truly,
Tom Crown, Human Resources Director

151. Who will Mr. Yamaguchi be?
   (A) Job applicant
   (B) Reference
   (C) One of 32 laid-off employees
   (D) Human resources director

152. Why did Mr. Crown turn down an interview with a job applicant?
   (A) He couldn't take the chance because of a business trip.
   (B) The applicant was not remarkable enough to be hired.
   (C) Hiring a new person was not proper due to the dismissal of 32 employees.
   (D) The company couldn't afford a salary because of its financial difficulties.

GO ON TO THE NEXT PAGE

Questions 153-154 refer to the following advertisement.

**Why Advertise with Nifty?**
The #1 activity of Internet users is using an e-mail service, and Nifty is the premier e-mail application.

How Long do Nifty Users Spend Time on E-mail Services Everyday?

Less than an hour - 35%

2 hours - 25%                    3 hours - 9%

4 hours - 21%                    More than 4 hours - 10%

Source : Nifty download survey, March 2014

Marketability
   Advertisers can target groups of Nifty users.

Dependability
   - Each advertisement showed for at least a full 100 seconds, guaranteed!
   - No competitive environment
   - Advertisements show up even when the Nifty user is using e-mail offline

Accountability
   - Dedicated Advertisement Server
   - 100% developed and managed by PROCOME
   - Perfect advertiser accountability via certified affidavit
   - Password protected advertiser access to advertisement server web site, for monitoring
     campaign progress state

153. According to the advertisement, what is the most popular action for internet users?
   (A) Advertising their products on Nifty web-site
   (B) E-mailing
   (C) Buying discounted goods from the internet shopping mall
   (D) Taking benefits of using Nifty e-mail

154. What is NOT a benefit of advertising with Nifty?
   (A) Guaranteed advertising time
   (B) Advertisements still show up for offline users.
   (C) Non stop ads rotating even without mouse movement
   (D) No competition

---

### Roses for Mom

$45.50 (valued at : $50.00)
You are able to choose your delivery date!

Sunday & Mother's Day Charges :
   An additional $10.50 fee for Sunday delivery
   An additional $5.50 fee for Mother's day

If you order this service, you will receive a free Glass Vase. You can select the color of the vase. There will be a range of colors shown as an option on the order summary page. Gorgeous, vibrant, fresh roses are perfect for showing mom how special she really is. These beautiful flowers are shipped fresh, budding, and ready to bloom in order for them to last much longer.

Includes an assortment of 20 Roses. Flowers are hand-picked and tied, then shipped directly from our flower farm along with your personal message.

---

**155.** Who is this advertisement directed toward?
(A) People who want to buy glass vases for a party
(B) People who take lessons in flower arrangement
(C) People who own gardens surrounded by tulips
(D) People who wish to make their moms happy on Mother's day

**156.** How much should a person who wants to purchase roses pay on Mother's day?
(A) $45.50
(B) $51.00
(C) $55.50
(D) $56.00

**157.** According to the advertisement, what does this shop do so the roses will remain fresh?
(A) Roses are delivered by a door to door service.
(B) The shop staff grows flowers themselves.
(C) The staff always sends roses just about to bloom.
(D) Only fresh and beautiful roses are transported to customers.

*GO ON TO THE NEXT PAGE*

**SB Coffee Care Cafe**

25 Lafayette Avenue
Chicago, WA 93728
Tel: (308) 332-5324
Fax: (308) 332-0694
E-mail: carecoffee@cafe.com

Chris Russel
Credit Manager
SB Coffee House, Ltd
643 Chatley Road
Jacksonville, IL 997432

Dear Mr. Russel:

I would like to thank you for opening an account with us. As one of the leading managers in this industry, we can assure you that our services and our products will not disappoint your needs.

I want to take this opportunity to briefly set forth our terms and conditions for maintaining an open account with our company. You must pay invoices within 20 days of receiving it, and a 5% discount is available if your payment is paid within 15 days. We consider this incentive a great opportunity for our clients to increase their profit margin and therefore encourage the use of this discount whenever possible. However, we require that you pay our invoices within the specified time, for our clients to take advantage of this 5% discount privilege. This discount is valid only for regular-priced products.

Many times throughout the year we may provide our clients with additional discounts on our goods. To determine your cost, you should apply your special discount first and then calculate your 5% discount for an early payment.

As the credit manager, I am pleased to answer any questions you may have about your new account. I can be reached at the above number. (308) 332-5324. Thank you.

Yours sincerely,

Edwin Conley
Credit manager of SB Coffee Care Cafe

**158.** Why is this letter written?

(A) To apply to the credit manager
(B) To open a new account
(C) To describe the discount policy
(D) To get a discount

**159.** What is mentioned about SB Coffee House, Ltd?

(A) Money is payable within 20 days of receiving it.
(B) 2% discount will be given every month.
(C) The prices of the coffee products
(D) The company has been established a year ago.

**160.** Which of the following is TRUE about this letter?

(A) Edwin Conley's e-mail address is carecoffee@cafe.com.
(B) The credit manager is fussy and will not answer any questions.
(C) The letter is written to Coffee Care Cafo.
(D) Julia Krinard's phone number is tel: (206) 283-8485.

*GO ON TO THE NEXT PAGE*

Have you always hoped to invest, but didn't know where to get started? --- [1] ---. We're here today to provide you with 3 fundamental guidelines to investing wisely for your future. The first step is to have clear objectives. Decide how long you will invest for, and what your needs will be in the future. --- [2] ---. The second step is to understand the range of possibilities. You'll want a varied portfolio: one combined with stocks, mutual funds, bonds, and cash. Each of these items have different risks associated with them and also diversified potential rewards. Make sure you understand this before you purchase, so there won't be any big risks later. Finally, the third step is to have realistic anticipations. As our friend Leonardo da Vinci said in the year 1500: "Anyone who wants to be rich in only a day will be hanged in a year."

--- [3] ---. For the past several years, New York stocks have averaged 25% in annual returns, but you shouldn't expect this return to continue. Since the year 2000, stocks have averaged in a 13% annual return, it's unpredictable and there are also many minus years. --- [4] ---. You must stay in for a long period of time and weather the storm, while not being too greedy.

**161.** The word "objectives" in line 6, is closest in meaning to

(A) ways
(B) purposes
(C) efforts
(D) options

**162.** Why should people invest in a long term?

(A) The market has both up and down years.
(B) You can earn bigger guaranteed returns.
(C) 30% returns can be achieved with the right stocks.
(D) The contract is written that way.

**163.** In which of the positions marked [1], [2], [3] and [4] does the following sentence best belong?

"Therefore, you must not hurry in investing."

(A) [1]
(B) [2]
(C) [3]
(D) [4]

*GO ON TO THE NEXT PAGE*

**Questions 164-167** refer to the following online chat discussion.

| Online Chat | _ □ × |
|---|---|

**Martin Berg** — 11:30 A.M.

Greetings everybody. For our Riverside outlet we need to make a new spring menu item by Wednesday. What state are the plans at right now?

**Edmond Whitney** — 11:31 A.M.

We have five choices. It is so difficult to narrow them down.

**Jessie Terrel** — 11:32 A.M.

Sure, but the flavors aren't popular among the diners who've sampled them.

**Martin Berg** — 11:33 A.M.

That really isn't so important. It will only be on sale for a few weeks. It is just meant to be an exciting item that makes people talk about us.

**Kory Petty** — 11:35 A.M.

Yes, but we don't want negative publicity because of products that taste bad, right?

**Edmond Whitney** — 11:37 A.M.

A lot of people liked non-fried food. It was a crowd favorite.

**Martin Berg** — 11:40 A.M.

That sounds good. But it isn't exciting. We need a really surprising combination.

**Jessie Terrel** — 11:44 A.M.

In that case, the idea that the diners we interviewed found most entertaining was called an ice-cream pie cake.

**Martin Berg** — 11:45 A.M.

Wow. What's that?

**Kory Petty** — 11:46 A.M.

It's a dessert.It's a pie baked inside a cake that is covered in ice-cream. It is really hard to eat.

**Martin Berg** — 11:49 A.M.

Sounds perfect! People will talk about it all the more. Make sure you send me a plan before the deadline. We need to get started on a campaign.

| | Send | ⌄ |

30

164. Where will the new product most likely be sold?

(A) At a hardware shop
(B) At an outlet
(C) At a restaurant
(D) At an electronics shop

165. At 11:40 A.M., why does Mr. Berg say "That sounds good"?

(A) To consider Mr. Whitney idea
(B) To check the client's need
(C) To express approval of the idea
(D) To choose one item from a selection

166. What does Mr. Kory Petty express concern about?

(A) Continuation of the company's fame
(B) Missing the deadline
(C) Getting a project's budget
(D) Completing a sales target

167. According to Mr. Martin Berg, what is the most important consideration?

(A) Establishing an entertaining campaign slogan
(B) Inspiring conversation about the company's product
(C) Replacing the product's ingredients with healthier alternatives
(D) Reducing the cost of less profitable items

GO ON TO THE NEXT PAGE

Beta Crane Company
4231 East North Avenue
Texas, IL 22003

June 21, 2023

Sandra Farcon
American Commercial Attach
South West Region
U.S. Embassy Offices, Suite 1022
Millan, Italy

Dear Ashley:

I hope that all businesses are well in Cairo. It's been a while since I last talked with you and Mr. Lim. I think that the time for a well-deserved vacation has finally come, but, unfortunately, I won't be enjoying my vacation time. I'm sure you and Mr. Lim feel the same way, but you know how business can be.

Ashley, Beta has had some recent problems that have come to my immediate attention. We have a shipment of ten cranes that were expected to be shipped on July 1st. I placed the order in March, but we still have not received them. Raymond tried to make arrangements with Melvin Cransey, the supervisor of the ICO bureau of the Saudi Royal Ministry of Construction and Land Management, to help speed up the approval process. Unfortunately, I think we won't get much help from her. With Ramadan coming soon, I think that it will be very hard to process this business, so we have to work fast before employees leave to spend times with their families. The Production Manager is worried about this shipment and there is a total of 30 cranes that have been ordered by AK Equipment. They're expected to receive 10 cranes continuously until September 22.

I want you to help to speed up government approval. I really appreciate everything you've done for Beta in the past. I think you will agree that we need to help the U.S. government retain good relations with this country since business has been very successful in this country.

I'm leaving for Cairo on Monday to have a meeting with some officials to deal with another business. I want to get together with you as quickly as possible when I arrive, so we can hopefully get this matter taken care of. I'll be staying at the Hotel Nikki in Cairo. If you want to talk to me before I leave, I'll be in my office late this evening, or you can reach my cellular phone number: 010-24-332-7556-4535. I look forward to meeting you soon.

Sincerely,
John Delpart

168. What is Delpart asking for Ashley to do?

(A) Help speed up the approval process
(B) Take a vacation
(C) Maintain good relationships
(D) Order more cranes

169. When did Delpart write this letter?

(A) February 1, 2023
(B) July 1, 2023
(C) August 11, 2023
(D) June 21, 2023

170. How many cranes did the AK Equipment order?

(A) 1
(B) 5
(C) 10
(D) 30

171. I low could Ms. Ashley contact Mr. Delpart before she leaves for Cairo?

(A) By letter
(B) By e-mail
(C) By phone
(D) By cable

GO ON TO THE NEXT PAGE

## 2024 Benefit Package Notice

Medical / Dental Insurance
Employees have the opportunity to register for a dental insurance plan and either a PPO (Preferred Provider Option) or an EPO (Exclusive Provider Option) medical plan. --- [1] ---.

Life Insurance: Employees can register in a group term life insurance program. The insurance coverage is equal to one and one half times the annual wage of employees and the County pays for 75% of the premium. --- [2] ---.

Voluntary Group Life insurance: Employees and their life partners can purchase additional life insurance at group prices. Their children may also be included in the coverage. --- [3] ---.

Long-Term Disability Insurance: The County pays the whole premium for long-term disability insurance. Employees should work at least 70% of their work time to be eligible for the benefit. --- [4] ---.

Employee Assistance Program: The Employee Assistance Program provides clients with a complimentary, confidential counseling and referral service program devised to help employees and their families deal with personal issues.

Pretax Benefit Program: This program permits you to use before-tax wage dollars to pay for the County's dental and medical premiums and certain health and dependent care (day care) costs.

Credit Union: All County employees are eligible to join the Toronto Employees Federal Credit Union.

Contact Toronto County Human Resources at 394-530-4022 with questions about benefits.
Phone : General Information 394-530-4063
         Non-Emergency 394-530-4032
         Emergency 119

172. What is this notice about?

    (A) To introduce County Human
        Resources
    (B) To introduce the payment of the
        employees' annual salary
    (C) To introduce the negative effects of
        medicine overdose
    (D) To introduce a benefits package

173. Who is able to join the Voluntary Group
     Life Insurance?

    (A) A companion
    (B) A consort
    (C) A cousin
    (D) A colleague

174. What is NOT true about this notice?

    (A) Employees could join either a PPO or
        an EPO.
    (B) The County pays all the Long-Term
        Disability Insurance fee.
    (C) The County pays three quarters of
        the Life Insurance fee.
    (D) The Employee Assistance Program
        charges for a counseling service.

175. In which of the positions marked [1], [2],
     [3] and [4] does the following sentence
     best belong?

     "He/she also has the opportunity to
     register his/her family in the group
     insurance program."

    (A) [1]
    (B) [2]
    (C) [3]
    (D) [4]

GO ON TO THE NEXT PAGE

Dear Ms. Williams,

The person identified below is being considered for employment and has signed a statement authorizing this verification and investigation. We would like to hear your opinions and thoughts.

Name of Applicant : Heather Jackson
Social Security Number : 337-789-8686
Dates of Employment : April, 2019 ~ May, 2024
Position Last Held : Executive Secretary
Final Rate of Payment : $40.00 per hour
Is the above information correct?   Yes, _____      No, _____
If not, please make corrections.  _____
What is your opinion as to this person?

    Ability : _____        Effort : _____
      Conduct : _____       Attendance  : _____

Reason for leaving your company : _____

Thank you very much for your assistance.

Sincerely.
Steve Anderson
Human Resources Manager, Torr Financial

---

Dear Mr. Anderson,

I am enclosing the Employment Verification Form you have sent me for Minky Giles.

Name of Applicant : Heather Jackson
Social Security Number : 337-789-8686
Dates of Employment : April, 2019 ~ May, 2024
Position Last Held : Executive Secretary
Final Rate of Payment : $40.00 per hour

Is the above information correct?  Yes, _____  No, ___X___
If not, please make corrections :  _Her final rate of payment was $45.00 per hour._

What is your opinion as to this person?
Ability :  _Excellent secretarial skills_      Effort :  _Hard worker_
Conduct :  _Focused and organized_    Attendance :  _Near perfect_

Reason for leaving your company :  _She had to relocate._

**176.** When did Heather Jackson start working at her previous company?

(A) April, 2019
(B) May, 2019
(C) March, 2024
(D) May, 2024

**177.** What was the position Heather Jackson held at her last company?

(A) Financial analyst
(B) Human Resources assistant director
(C) Marketing manager
(D) Executive Secretary

**178.** What is Steve Anderson's job title?

(A) Internal Investigator
(B) Human Resources Manager
(C) Executive Secretary
(D) Accounting manager

**179.** What was the final rate of payment for Heather Jackson at her old job?

(A) $40.00 per hour
(B) $45.00 per hour
(C) $40,000 per year
(D) $45,000 per year

**180.** What was Ms. Williams' opinion of Heather's ability?

(A) She is good at organizing.
(B) She is a hard worker.
(C) She has nearly perfect attendance.
(D) She has excellent secretarial skills.

*GO ON TO THE NEXT PAGE*

**Questions 181-185** refer to the following two e-mails.

To : All New Age Software Division Heads
From : Kenny Logan, CEO
Sub : Mandatory Meeting

SCHEDULE CHANGE ANNOUNCEMENT

Please be aware of the fact that, due to holidays, our biannual new product development team meeting scheduled for Wednesday, December 15th, will be canceled. The date has been rescheduled for the preceding Monday. Attendance at this meeting is mandatory, so please be sure to adjust your schedules accordingly. Courtney Ross will be giving a presentation on new products expected to be unveiled by our competitors early next year.

| To | Kenny Logan |
|---|---|
| From | Jack Arnold, Sales Division Chief |
| Subject | Re: Meeting Rescheduling |

Dear Kenny Logan,

Because there was a sudden change in scheduling for the meeting, I was really surprised. I realized that attendance to these meetings is required, but that Wednesday my son is scheduled to have back surgery. I had my vacation approved two weeks ago. However, I have already gotten in touch with Courtney, and she will be e-mailing me her presentation notes and I have asked Bill Hanks to sit in for me on the presentation day.

Jack Arnold

181. Why was the meeting moved forward?

    (A) An operation
    (B) The National holidays
    (C) To respond to rival companies
        activities
    (D) Because of the weather

182. How often are these meetings held?

    (A) Once a year
    (B) Once a month
    (C) Twice a year
    (D) Three times a year

183. Who is supposed to attend the meeting?

    (A) Department managers
    (B) Heads of state
    (C) All employees
    (D) Software buyers

184. Why can't Jack Arnold attend the
     meeting?

    (A) He will be in the hospital.
    (B) He is taking a two-week vacation.
    (C) His son is going to have back
        surgery.
    (D) Bill Hanks is replacing him.

185. What did Jack Arnold do with respect to
     Courtney Ross?

    (A) He contacted her directly.
    (B) He asked Tom Hardy to call her.
    (C) He gave her his business card.
    (D) He contacted her to give the
        presentation.

GO ON TO THE NEXT PAGE

Innovative Cards, Ltd. is well known to many customers for making perfect business cards. You can find hundreds of unique designs on our website, www.innovtivecardsltd.net. Choose your preferred styles, and we will deliver 20-card sets directly to your office without shipping fees. Our premium paper stock is three times thicker than typical business cards found in print shops and comes in either matte or glossy finish, allowing you to stand out in your field so you can effortlessly start conversations and make a great impression. When you have decided on the cards that are right for you, just order your preferred design and paper on online, and we will send them out to you within a few days, or for expedited delivery, overnight for an additional fee.

### www.innovtivecards.net/placeorder

Order Number : #56101
Client : Jenna Blackstone

| Design | Code | Finish | Quantity | Price | etc. |
|--------|------|--------|----------|-------|------|
| Minimal | DD019 | glossy | 20 | free | |
| Bold Arcs | DD199 | glossy | 20 | free | |
| Vintage | DD160 | matte | 20 | free | |
| Brushstroke | DD046 | matte | 100 | $49.99 | reorder |
| Sales Tax | | | | | 5% |
| Expedited Shipping | | | | | |
| Total | | | | | |

Confirm and proceed to payment

| To | Customer Satisfaction Center <cs@innovtivecards.net> |
|---|---|
| From | Jenna Blackstone <jennablackstone@msn.com> |
| Date | May 6 |
| Subject | Re : Order Number #56101 |

To Customer Satisfaction Center

Hi. We are so grateful for your rapid delivery of my order #56101. It arrived yesterday. Unfortunately, one sample was missing from my order. I had requested DD160 but it wasn't in the envelope. DD019, DD 199, and DD046 were included, so DD160 must have just been overlooked. Could you send me my original requested design, as well as additional samples that are comparable to it? That one seemed to match our company's new logo well: the others were too bright for it.

Thank you very much in advance.

Jenna Blackstone

186. Who will be interested in the advertisement?

(A) Those who are searching for their appropriate business card
(B) Those who want unique designs on their web-site
(C) Those who are finding their favorite designs
(D) Those who want to give a great impression to their customer

187. According to the advertisement, what are the customers advised to do?

(A) Drop by a print shop to compare designs
(B) Require paper stock only
(C) Order several varieties
(D) Compose their own designs

188. What can be inferred about order number #56101?

(A) It contained three samples.
(B) It was sent on May 6.
(C) It has 20-card set which Ms. Jenna Blackstone bought.
(D) It arrived within one business day.

189. Which of the following will Ms. Jenna Blackstone like?

(A) Minimal
(B) Bold Arcs
(C) Vintage
(D) Brushstroke

190. What problem does Ms. Jenna Blackstone mention about her order?

(A) She didn't get one item.
(B) The quality was bad.
(C) It took a long time to process the order.
(D) She was charged too much.

GO ON TO THE NEXT PAGE

**Questions 191-195** refer to the following schedule, survey and review.

## Schedule of Tour in Rome

| Day 1st | 6 March 2022 | Welcome to Rome<br>We will gather at our hotel in Rome at 4 P.M. for a short meeting and orientation. Then, we will get acquainted with one another over a "Welcome to Rome" dinner together. |
|---|---|---|
| Day 2nd | 7 March 2022 | The Historic Heart of Rome<br>Your guide will lead a walking tour of the city, including visits to the world's most famous church, Piazza San Pietro. Then, we will take a walk through the Vatican Museums, with free time for lunch on your own. We will end our afternoon at the Colosseum, where after an introduction, you will be free to enjoy the tour of the historical site on your own. |
| Day 3rd | 8 March 2022 | Piazza Navona<br>In the morning, we will take the Metro, then walk up Piazza Navona to tour the colorful neighborhood. We'll end our walk at the magnificent views of Rome from three fountains of Fiumi, Nettuno, and Moro. You'll be free for lunch and have time to explore more of the city on your own this afternoon. We'll group again in the evening to enjoy a wine tasting and dinner together before going on a romantic Tevere River cruise |
| Day 4th | 9 March 2022 | Tour over After Breakfast<br>Breakfast is provided, but there are no group activities today. We'll head to Leonardo Da Vinch International Airport by shuttle bus. |

\* Schedule specifics subject to change.

## E & F Tour
## Tourists Survey Form

We are very much interested in your comments and suggestions regarding our tours. Please take a few moments to answer the following questions. The results of this evaluation will be used to improve our future tours. Did this tour meet your expectations in the following areas?

| | Very Bad | Bad | Middle | Good | Very Good |
|---|---|---|---|---|---|
| Transportation | ○ | ○ | ● | ○ | ○ |
| Hotel | ○ | ○ | ○ | ○ | ● |
| Activities | ○ | ○ | ● | ○ | ○ |
| Guide | ○ | ○ | ○ | ● | ○ |
| Meals | ○ | ● | ○ | ○ | ○ |
| Overall services | ○ | ○ | ○ | ● | ○ |

I was very unlucky and wasn't able to attend the reception dinner because I got sick and had to stay in bed. The tour would have been a lot more fun if I had been able to join the dinner and had had a chance to get to know the other participants. I wish the guide had arranged an opportunity to introduce me to the other members. However, overall, I was quite happy about the tour. The hotel we stayed at was especially well above my expectations.

Gerry Benning

191. What can be inferred from the schedule?

(A) All tourists will have no chance to take a subway
(B) There can be a possibility of a change.
(C) All meals will be included in the tour.
(D) There is no special event on the 4th day of the tour.

192. What is the last activity of this tour?

(A) A visit to a church
(B) A visit to a museum
(C) A wine tasting and dinner
(D) A river cruise

193. Why does E & F Tour make a survey for the tourists?

(A) To offer information on the tour
(B) To answer questions from the customers
(C) To meet the tourists' needs
(D) To enhance the quality of the future tour

194. Which of the following was Mr. Gerry Benning most dissatisfied with?

(A) Transportation
(B) Accommodation
(C) Guide
(D) Meals

195. Which of the following didn't Mr. Gerry Benning participant in?

(A) An orientation
(B) The Historic Heart of Rome
(C) Walking up Piazza Navona
(D) Enjoying a wine tasting and dinner

GO ON TO THE NEXT PAGE

## Hilltop Tents

| Model | Size | Color | Price |
|---|---|---|---|
| Hilltop Castle 2 | 2 people | Red/Yellow | $129 |
| Hilltop Castle 4 | 4 people | Red/Yellow | $219 |
| Hilltop Castle 6 | 6 people | Blue/Green | $329 |
| Hilltop Castle 8 | 8 people | Blue/Green | $419 |

**Description**

Made for the harsh weather conditions, Hilltop Castle products are ideal for large families camping in the high mountainous area.

» Two rooms with a center divider

» Two large doors with four zipper sliders

» Cutting-edge weather resistant material

» ultra-lightweight, titanium tents stakes

May 15

We purchased the Hilltop Castle 4 in blue for our family trips. Overall, we are a bit disappointed. First, the tent is not quite big enough for our family of three. Second, we have had some problems with the zippers. A couple of them are permanently stuck in one place, so now we can only use the doors on the side of the tent.

Moreover, I am worried that the tent's stakes are unable to handle high winds, as they are so lightweight. I am sometimes concerned that the tent is in danger of blowing away.

Wesley Holliday

We regret to hear about your inconvenience with our product. Unexpectedly you received a defective product, so we will send you a replacement. In addition, as a token of apology for having caused you with this issue, we will send you a larger model without additional charge. However, it is not available in the color you have now. Note that in order for us to send you the replacement, you will need to e-mail us proof of your purchase.

As for your concerns regarding our tent stakes, rest assured that they are entirely sturdy. Though they are made of lightweight material, we have proven their strength and effectiveness in several trials.

Lowell Bollman

Hilltop Tents Customer Satisfaction Center

**196.** According to the information, which of the following is true NOT about Hilltop tents?

(A) High durability
(B) Maximized use of space
(C) Convenient access
(D) Blocks ultraviolet rays

**197.** What problem doesn't Ms. Wesley Holliday mention?

(A) The Hilltop Castle 4 is too small for her family.
(B) The Hilltop Castle 4 has a broken zipper.
(C) The Hilltop Castle 4 is not colorful.
(D) The Hilltop Castle 4 is too light for the wind.

**198.** Which product does Mr. Lowell Bollman offer to Ms. Wesley Holliday?

(A) Hilltop Castle 2
(B) Hilltop Castle 4
(C) Hilltop Castle 6
(D) Hilltop Castle 8

**199.** What should Ms. Wesley Bollman do to receive a replacement?

(A) She should complete a return form.
(B) She should send a copy of her receipt.
(C) She should prove the flaw of her tent.
(D) She should send the defective tent to the company.

**200.** In the e-mail, the word "issue", line 3, paragraph 1, is closest in meaning to

(A) matter
(B) conflict
(C) edition
(D) copy

**Stop! This is the end of the test. If you finish before time is called, you may go back to Parts 5, 6, and 7 and check your work.**

GO ON TO THE NEXT PAGE

MEMO

MEMO

토익
실전모의고사
SET #1 정답

| | 응시일 | TEST 소요시간 | 맞은 개수 | 환산 점수 |
|---|---|---|---|---|
| LC | ___월 ___일 | _____ 분 | _____ 개 | _____ 점 |
| RC | | _____ 분 | _____ 개 | _____ 점 |

| PART 1 | PART 2 | PART 3 | | PART 4 | PART 5 | PART 6 | PART 7 | | |
|---|---|---|---|---|---|---|---|---|---|
| 1 (A) | 7 (C) | 32 (D) | 62 (B) | 71 (D) | 101 (B) | 131 (C) | 147 (D) | 176 (A) | 186 (A) |
| 2 (C) | 8 (A) | 33 (B) | 63 (C) | 72 (C) | 102 (A) | 132 (D) | 148 (A) | 177 (D) | 187 (C) |
| 3 (A) | 9 (C) | 34 (B) | 64 (A) | 73 (B) | 103 (C) | 133 (B) | 149 (A) | 178 (B) | 188 (D) |
| 4 (A) | 10 (C) | 35 (D) | 65 (C) | 74 (A) | 104 (C) | 134 (D) | 150 (D) | 179 (B) | 189 (C) |
| 5 (D) | 11 (A) | 36 (A) | 66 (A) | 75 (D) | 105 (A) | 135 (C) | 151 (B) | 180 (D) | 190 (A) |
| 6 (B) | 12 (A) | 37 (B) | 67 (B) | 76 (C) | 106 (A) | 136 (C) | 152 (C) | 181 (B) | 191 (B) |
| | 13 (C) | 38 (C) | 68 (B) | 77 (C) | 107 (C) | 137 (D) | 153 (B) | 182 (C) | 192 (D) |
| | 14 (B) | 39 (B) | 69 (D) | 78 (A) | 108 (B) | 138 (C) | 154 (C) | 183 (A) | 193 (D) |
| | 15 (A) | 40 (A) | 70 (C) | 79 (D) | 109 (C) | 139 (C) | 155 (D) | 184 (C) | 194 (D) |
| | 16 (A) | 41 (D) | | 80 (A) | 110 (B) | 140 (D) | 156 (B) | 185 (A) | 195 (A) |
| | 17 (C) | 42 (C) | | 81 (D) | 111 (A) | 141 (B) | 157 (C) | | 196 (D) |
| | 18 (A) | 43 (B) | | 82 (C) | 112 (D) | 142 (D) | 158 (C) | | 197 (C) |
| | 19 (C) | 44 (D) | | 83 (C) | 113 (B) | 143 (C) | 159 (A) | | 198 (C) |
| | 20 (B) | 45 (C) | | 84 (B) | 114 (A) | 144 (C) | 160 (A) | | 199 (B) |
| | 21 (C) | 46 (C) | | 85 (A) | 115 (A) | 145 (A) | 161 (B) | | 200 (A) |
| | 22 (A) | 47 (B) | | 86 (A) | 116 (B) | 146 (D) | 162 (A) | | |
| | 23 (B) | 48 (D) | | 87 (D) | 117 (D) | | 163 (D) | | |
| | 24 (B) | 49 (A) | | 88 (A) | 118 (A) | | 164 (C) | | |
| | 25 (C) | 50 (D) | | 89 (B) | 119 (D) | | 165 (C) | | |
| | 26 (A) | 51 (A) | | 90 (B) | 120 (D) | | 166 (A) | | |
| | 27 (B) | 52 (B) | | 91 (A) | 121 (C) | | 167 (B) | | |
| | 28 (A) | 53 (B) | | 92 (D) | 122 (D) | | 168 (A) | | |
| | 29 (A) | 54 (D) | | 93 (B) | 123 (C) | | 169 (D) | | |
| | 30 (B) | 55 (A) | | 94 (A) | 124 (B) | | 170 (D) | | |
| | 31 (A) | 56 (D) | | 95 (C) | 125 (C) | | 171 (C) | | |
| | | 57 (A) | | 96 (B) | 126 (D) | | 172 (D) | | |
| | | 58 (B) | | 97 (D) | 127 (A) | | 173 (B) | | |
| | | 59 (D) | | 98 (C) | 128 (B) | | 174 (D) | | |
| | | 60 (C) | | 99 (B) | 129 (B) | | 175 (A) | | |
| | | 61 (A) | | 100 (D) | 130 (B) | | | | |

퀵
토익 SET
#2
실전모의고사

LC 음원

채점 &
정답 및 해설

지금부터 Actual Test를 진행합니다.
실제 시험과 동일한 방식으로 진행됨을 말씀드리며,
LC 음원은 QR코드로 청취할 수 있습니다.

준비되면 바로 시작하세요!

## LISTENING TEST

In the Listening test, you will be asked to demonstrate how well you understand spoken English. The entire Listening test will last approximately 45 minutes. There are four parts, and directions are given for each part. You must mark your answers on the separate answer sheet. Do not write your answers in your test book.

## PART 1

**Directions:** For each question in this part, you will hear four statements about a picture in your test book. When you hear the statements, you must select the one statement that best describes what you see in the picture. Then find the number of the question on your answer sheet and mark your answer. The statements will not be printed in your test book and will be spoken only one time.

Statment (A), "Some people are paddling through the water," is the best description of the picture, so you should select answer (A) and mark it on your answer sheet.

1.

2.

*GO ON TO THE NEXT PAGE* ➡

3.

4.

**5.**

**6.**

*GO ON TO THE NEXT PAGE* →

**Directions:** You will hear a question or statement and three responses spoken in English. They will not be printed in your test book and will be spoken only one time. Select the best response to the question or statement and mark the letter (A), (B), or (C) on your answer sheet.

7. Mark your answer on your answer sheet.

8. Mark your answer on your answer sheet.

9. Mark your answer on your answer sheet.

10. Mark your answer on your answer sheet.

11. Mark your answer on your answer sheet.

12. Mark your answer on your answer sheet.

13. Mark your answer on your answer sheet.

14. Mark your answer on your answer sheet.

15. Mark your answer on your answer sheet.

16. Mark your answer on your answer sheet.

17. Mark your answer on your answer sheet.

18. Mark your answer on your answer sheet.

19. Mark your answer on your answer sheet.

20. Mark your answer on your answer sheet.

21. Mark your answer on your answer sheet.

22. Mark your answer on your answer sheet.

23. Mark your answer on your answer sheet.

24. Mark your answer on your answer sheet.

25. Mark your answer on your answer sheet.

26. Mark your answer on your answer sheet.

27. Mark your answer on your answer sheet.

28. Mark your answer on your answer sheet.

29. Mark your answer on your answer sheet.

30. Mark your answer on your answer sheet.

31. Mark your answer on your answer sheet.

## PART 3

**Directions:** You will hear some conversations between two or more people. You will be asked to answer three questions about what the speakers say in each conversation. Select the best response to each question and mark the letter (A), (B), (C), or (D) on your answer sheet. The conversations will not be printed in your test book and will be spoken only one time.

32. What did the man receive in the e-mail?
    (A) List of properties
    (B) The properties owner's phone number
    (C) The e-mail address of Tracy Green
    (D) The agreement of a lease

33. What does the man require?
    (A) Enough parking space
    (B) Less noise
    (C) Easy access to public transportation
    (D) Convenient amenities

34. What does the woman say she will do next?
    (A) Contact the property owner.
    (B) Visit Mr. Stan Hall's office.
    (C) Request the tenant to open the apartment.
    (D) Send the owner a contract.

35. What is being constructed?
    (A) WWP Broadcasting
    (B) The New South River Bridge
    (C) Local call center
    (D) The International Trade building

36. What difficulty does the man mention?
    (A) The weather caused a halt in the construction.
    (B) It wasn't convenient to go to the construction site.
    (C) The construction procedure was proceeding too fast.
    (D) Too many people expected the bridge to be open to traffic in November.

37. When will the project most likely be finished?
    (A) April
    (B) May
    (C) October
    (D) November

38. Where most likely will the speakers be working at?
    (A) At a hospital
    (B) At the culture center
    (C) At a fitness center
    (D) At a school

39. What does the woman agree to do?
    (A) To share with all of her employees
    (B) To know the feedback
    (C) To compile the clients' comments
    (D) To request more benefits

40. What does the man talk about with the instructors?
    (A) Finding their trends and feedback
    (B) Offering additional fees
    (C) Increasing their weekday hours
    (D) Instructing yoga classes to members

41. According to the woman, what has recently happened?
    (A) She began her new job.
    (B) Her company joined with another company.
    (C) She became a director.
    (D) Her duty was changed in the company.

42. Why does the man say, "You don't say"?
    (A) To show a surprise
    (B) To agree on the woman's opinion.
    (C) To ask the woman not to leave the company.
    (D) To express another idea.

43. What problem does the man mention about the new management?
    (A) It began the new business.
    (B) It provides a safe work environment for him.
    (C) It knows all of the workers' thoughts.
    (D) It operates the company differently.

*GO ON TO THE NEXT PAGE*

44. What is the purpose of man's call?

    (A) To introduce World Tour Magazine to Ms. Glenn
    (B) To offer a work assignment
    (C) To request Ms. Glenn to subscribe
    (D) To announce the review of Ms. Glenn's article

45. What does the woman ask the man about?

    (A) The due date
    (B) The information on the Far East
    (C) The tour route
    (D) The subject of his article

46. What change does the man mention?

    (A) His pride as a freelancer writer
    (B) The content of the issue
    (C) The experience of Japan and Korea
    (D) A higher rate

47. What job is the woman interviewing for?

    (A) The customer director
    (B) The architect
    (C) The senior accountant
    (D) The head manager

48. According to the woman, what was the responsibility at her previous job?

    (A) She provided some information for the tenants.
    (B) She maintained and repaired the building.
    (C) She managed the leasing firm.
    (D) She was the owner of the largest accounting firm.

49. How does the woman know Emilias Railey?

    (A) She worked with Emilias Railey as a partner.
    (B) She knew Emilias Railey on the leasing firm.
    (C) She introduced Emilias Railey to her professor.
    (D) She was Emilias Railey's predecessor.

50. Why did the man call the woman?

    (A) To complain about the warranty
    (B) To apologize to her for the late shipment
    (C) To inform about a problem with some machines
    (D) To buy office equipment

51. What did the company receive last month?

    (A) Papers
    (B) Photocopiers
    (C) Printers
    (D) Descriptions

52. What will the woman probably do next?

    (A) Call another department
    (B) E-mail to her director
    (C) Cancel the order
    (D) Print color copies

53. What are the speakers discussing?

    (A) A job as a programmer
    (B) The abilities of artificial intelligence
    (C) A book written by a previous colleague
    (D) A copy machine

54. What does the man mean when he say, "I am so happy for her"?

    (A) He received advice from her book.
    (B) He wishes his friend good fortune.
    (C) He is pleased about his coworker's success.
    (D) He considered the book interesting.

55. What does the man indicate about the book?

    (A) He think it's unique.
    (B) He will buy it.
    (C) He has already ordered it.
    (D) He will lend it to her.

**56.** What did the woman ask Mr. Thompson to do?

(A) To repair her computer
(B) To collect his document
(C) To correct his paperwork
(D) To work with Mr. Chadwick

**57.** According to the woman, what will happen this morning?

(A) Ms. Dunbar will meet the customer.
(B) Mr. Thompson will revise his document.
(C) Mr. Chadwick will take part in the conference.
(D) Ms. Dunbar will read Mr. Thompson's report.

**58.** Where is Mr. Thompson's newest report?

(A) On Mr. Thompson's desk
(B) In Mr. Chadwick's file cabinet
(C) In other office
(D) Between Ms. Dunbar's files

---

**59.** Why is the woman calling?

(A) To check a grade
(B) To reserve a hotel
(C) To register for a course
(D) To apply for a membership

**60.** How can the woman get a discount?

(A) By coming on a weekday
(B) By referring beginners
(C) By arriving earlier
(D) By paying in advance

**61.** What will the woman do next?

(A) Enroll in the new class.
(B) Make a payment.
(C) Change the schedule.
(D) Open the website.

SPECIAL COUPON
for a valued guest

Sep. 1 ~ 7 ................................. 10% off
Sep. 8 ~ 15 ............................... 15% off
Sep. 16 ~ 23 ............................. 20% off
Sep. 24 ~ 30 ............................. 30% off

Based on check-in day !!!

Hillside Placid Hotel

**62.** Where does the woman work?

(A) At a restaurant
(B) At a hotel
(C) At a terminal
(D) At a station

**63.** What does the woman tell the man about?

(A) An extra luggage fee
(B) An estimate
(C) A discount policy
(D) A cancellation policy

**64.** Look at the graphic. How much will the man receive as a discount?

(A) 10%
(B) 15%
(C) 20%
(D) 30%

*GO ON TO THE NEXT PAGE*

## Position of Products

| Aisle 8 | Fruits and vegetables |
|---------|----------------------|
| Aisle 9 | Fish |
| Aisle 10 | Sauces and spices |
| Aisle 11 | Meat |

## Additional Fee

| Same day service | $200 |
|------------------|------|
| Next day service | $100 |
| One week service | $50 |
| One month service | $30 |

**65.** What does the woman ask the man about?

(A) Where a product promotion will be held
(B) Why a sale has finished so early
(C) If the sale is still being held
(D) When the tasting event will start

**66.** Look at the graphic. Where will the woman go first?

(A) To Aisle 8
(B) To Aisle 9
(C) To Aisle 10
(D) To Aisle 11

**67.** What does the man offer to do for the woman?

(A) To show a location
(B) To join the membership
(C) To recommend the cooking food
(D) To compare the various price

**68.** What kind of company will the woman most likely work at?

(A) An advertising company
(B) A Courier  service
(C) A printing office
(D) A hotel

**69.** Look at the graphic. How much will the man most likely pay for extra fees?

(A) $30
(B) $50
(C) $100
(D) $200

**70.** What will the man do next?

(A) Call an advertising company
(B) Try other company
(C) E-mail the order form
(D) Finish his document

## PART 4

**Directions:** You will hear some talks given by a single speaker. You will be asked to answer three questions about what the speakers say in each talk. Select the best response to each question and mark the letter (A), (B), (C), or (D) on your answer sheet. The talks will not be printed in your test book and will be spoken only one time.

71. What event is being planned?

(A) Lawrence Dingman's birthday party
(B) A private lesson
(C) A special occasion
(D) An anniversary dinner

72. What does the speaker mention about one of guests?

(A) He will be eighty years old now.
(B) He can go up and down the stairs.
(C) He will have to use a wheelchair.
(D) He will feel comfortable during the party.

73. What will the speaker want to receive?

(A) A list of ingredients of the menu items
(B) A cause of allergic reactions
(C) The location of the stairs
(D) The number of seats

74. What is being discussed?

(A) A great success
(B) A must-see
(C) A TV series
(D) A new theme

75. According to the speaker, what change will occur?

(A) An introduction program
(B) A top television station
(C) A plan to travel Asia
(D) A wider range of selection

76. What are listeners asked to do?

(A) To suggest a new concept
(B) To travel everywhere except Asia
(C) To watch the program
(D) To submit destinations

77. What is the topic of the reports?

(A) Traffic signs
(B) Bicycle rental program
(C) Housing policy
(D) Road construction

78. What is the concern of some Fordham residents?

(A) Super bikes will increase.
(B) People will move to another city.
(C) A walkway will be blocked.
(D) A vehicle will sell well.

79. According to the speaker, what will the mayor do tonight?

(A) Construct the streets
(B) Bring attention to him
(C) Write the address down
(D) Attend the meeting

80. Who is the Mr. Travis Gale?

(A) A popular entertainer
(B) An organizer of the country music events
(C) A news reporter
(D) An actor of many performances

81. What will be discussed on the program?

(A) Electronic tickets
(B) A drama at all the different venues
(C) The country music concert
(D) A rise in the cost for rent

82. What is the concert host considering?

(A) Identifying the spectators
(B) Solving customer affairs
(C) Introducing electronic tickets
(D) Changing to paper tickets

*GO ON TO THE NEXT PAGE*

83. What are the listeners going to do this morning?

    (A) Become models for the Med & Clothing company's advertising campaign

    (B) Announce a new line of spring clothes

    (C) Advertise campaign for medicine and clothing

    (D) Collect the Med & Clothing company's lines

84. What does the speaker say was learnt from a recent survey?

    (A) Some guests greatly appreciated the Med & Clothing company.

    (B) Many customers would like to be the actual models.

    (C) Some applicants complied with a survey.

    (D) Many people recognized the new spring collection.

85. What will the listeners receive?

    (A) A coupon worthy of $200

    (B) A right to take the photo

    (C) An ownership of a Med & Clothing store

    (D) A certificate of completion

86. Who is this announcement intended for?

    (A) Visitors

    (B) Factory workers

    (C) Delivery persons

    (D) Parking guides

87. According to the speaker, what will happen next week?

    (A) Some new machine will be delivered.

    (B) The parking lot will be renovated.

    (C) The office building will be closed.

    (D) The equipments will be repaired.

88. What are the listeners asked to do?

    (A) To keep the machine clean

    (B) To appreciate the cooperation

    (C) To help load the boxes

    (D) To park at a designated area

89. Where will the event take place?

    (A) At a convention room

    (B) At a stock market

    (C) At an exhibition site

    (D) At a trade fair

90. What does the high jump feature?

    (A) It competes with a stockman.

    (B) It includes food and drink.

    (C) It begins with a wood chopping event.

    (D) It is a event for domestic animals.

91. What does the woman mean, when she says "How exciting!"?

    (A) Many competitors will participate in the International Heritage Days Fair.

    (B) The International Heritage Days Fair is worth coming to.

    (C) The International Heritage Days Fair compromises all different events.

    (D) The International Heritage Days Fair is starting on April 15th.

92. According to the speaker, what will happen tonight?

    (A) A opening ceremony

    (B) A management meeting

    (C) An evening show

    (D) A coworker's retirement party

93. What does the speaker mention about Ms. Reed?

    (A) She has supported other employees.

    (B) She appreciated attending to tonight's banquet.

    (C) She would like to work in the accounting service department.

    (D) She spent more time in preparing tonight's banquet.

94. Why does the speaker say "Without further delay"?

    (A) She didn't offer any mail.

    (B) She has finished introducing a coworker.

    (C) She will talk to Ms. Reed on behalf of us.

    (D) She wants the listeners to bring it back.

| INFORMATION | |
| --- | --- |
| Group & Leader | Workload |
| One<br>Mr. Normand | Audio visual set up and operation |
| Two<br>Mr. Trinand | Cleanup and maintenance |
| Three<br>Ms. Windell | Beverage cart setup and operation |
| Four<br>Ms. Ignacio | Chairs and tables setup |

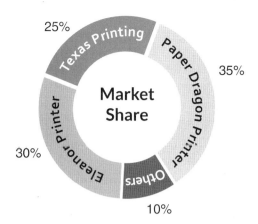

95. Where will the speaker probably work?

(A) At a library
(B) At a hospital
(C) At an auditorium
(D) At a museum

96. According to the talk, what are the listeners asked to do?

(A) To start with a different assignment
(B) To finish by a certain deadline
(C) To meet everyone's needs
(D) To complete their task to promote

97. Look at the graphic. Which group will be the last to leave the premises?

(A) Group One
(B) Group Two
(C) Group Three
(D) Group Four

98. What is the purpose of the report?

(A) A merger of two large companies
(B) An issue of Weekly Business News
(C) A launch of Eleanor Printer
(D) A cost of closing the Paper Dragon Printer

99. Look at the graphic. What would be the rank of Paper Dragon Printer early next year?

(A) First
(B) Second
(C) Third
(D) Fourth

100. According to the report, why will T & E be formed?

(A) To overcome market competition
(B) To help Paper Dragon Printer reduce its work
(C) To rank up in market share
(D) To concentrate on the domestic printing market

**This is the end of the Listening test. Turn to Part 5 in your text book.**

*GO ON TO THE NEXT PAGE*

# READING TEST

In the Reading test, you will read a variety of texts and answer several different types of reading comprehension questions. The entire Reading test will last 75 minutes. There are three parts, and directions are given for each part. You are encouraged to answer as many questions as possible within the time allowed.

You must mark your answers on the separate answer sheet. Do not write your answers in your test book.

# PART 5

**Directions:** A word or phrase is missing in each of the sentences below. Four answer choices are given below each sentence. Select the best answer to complete the sentence. Then mark the letter (A), (B), (C), or (D) on your answer sheet.

---

**101.** Because of the limited seating capacity of the conference room, ------- around one hundred people will be permitted to attend each training session.

(A) among
(B) only
(C) even
(D) between

**102.** Researchers must submit a written report at least two days ------- the deadline.

(A) after
(B) before
(C) upon
(D) to

**103.** The company has only received ten inquiries by phone since the extensive advertising campaign ran in last month's edition of the ------- magazine.

(A) shop
(B) shopped
(C) shopping
(D) shops

**104.** In order to meet the -------- need, Pierce Accounting Service tracks complex financial systems worldwide and therefore requires the most advanced computer technology.

(A) deficient
(B) satisfactory
(C) full
(D) immediate

**105.** A gift certificate offered by 21st Century Movie Co. is available at an ------- discount of $ 10.00 per ticket.

(A) add
(B) addition
(C) additional
(D) additionally

**106.** This week, all of the banks will be subjected to ------- testing of their balance sheets.

(A) exclusive
(B) enforced
(C) extensive
(D) combined

**107.** ------- who wish to apply for job openings in the accounting division should submit a resume to Human Resources by August 31st.

(A) Which
(B) One
(C) Those
(D) They

**108.** To thank our customers for their continued support, two ------- for future purchases will be provided.

(A) coupons
(B) tickets
(C) receipts
(D) invoices

109. Thanks to a revised -------, we at InterCom Inc. can provide you with free returns up to once a month.

(A) policy
(B) homepage
(C) procedure
(D) stage

110. Be a coordinator of a campus club and demonstrate leadership and communication skills as well as -------.

(A) responsible
(B) responsibly
(C) responsibility
(D) responsibilities

111. Employers use different forms of aptitude tests to assist ------- employee selection

(A) at
(B) on
(C) in
(D) to

112. Any employees can be qualified for incentives ------- they can finish their assignments on schedule.

(A) just as
(B) as though
(C) in order that
(D) insomuch as

113. The national bank's international payments network ------- to many countries around the world.

(A) results
(B) occurs
(C) stretches
(D) adapts

114. While your car ------- a part, maybe you can ask your colleague to take you to an auto mechanic.

(A) misses
(B) is missing
(C) has missed
(D) has been missing

115. Mr. Dan Furcal has ------- sold the old-fashioned vacuums, but I have two friends in the business who sell them.

(A) already
(B) still
(C) yet
(D) never

116. Library books that are checked out for more than 4 weeks will have an additional charge of ------- 10 dollars per item as a late fee.

(A) rough
(B) roughly
(C) roughness
(D) rougher

117. Using mobile devices during flights can interfere with transmission, so please turn them off ------- landing and taking off.

(A) while
(B) upon
(C) during
(D) meanwhile

118. Faculty members are expected to attend the annual seminar ------- they obtain their dean's written permission to be absent.

(A) if
(B) once
(C) unless
(D) as

119. To find out more about international shipping ------- , look at the attached guide visit our web-site.

(A) tolls
(B) fares
(C) values
(D) charges

120. The finance company is purchasing the advanced computer system, that is, the ------- edition to handle its investment portfolio.

(A) revised
(B) revising
(C) revises
(D) revise

*GO ON TO THE NEXT PAGE*

121. Our mailing list is available to carefully screened corporations whose ------- and services may interest you.
    (A) labor
    (B) union
    (C) management
    (D) products

122. International organizations have strongly criticized the Israeli crimes, ------- no action has been taken to stop these atrocities.
    (A) especially
    (B) however
    (C) consequently
    (D) moreover

123. All workers should notify their immediate supervisor before applying for their vacation two weeks ------- in advance.
    (A) much
    (B) so
    (C) very
    (D) well

124. If you need further information, please ------- our Customer Relations department to get the most up to date information or e-mail for a quick response.
    (A) send
    (B) transmit
    (C) contact
    (D) carry

125. Next week, I ------- Ms. Kelly McCarthy about her latest movie after her assistant explains its plot to me.
    (A) interview
    (B) am interviewing
    (C) have interviewed
    (D) will be interviewing

126. Beginning next month, drivers have to present at least two forms of their identification ------- they want to renew their outdated driver's licence.
    (A) whereas
    (B) provided that
    (C) because of
    (D) giving

127. The most popular mobile game on the market features some ------- ideas, easy functioning and fancy visual effects.
    (A) innovate
    (D) innovation
    (C) innovative
    (D) innovatively

128. As discussed in today's meeting, Tempa's newly elected mayor is taking a ------- fresh approach to improve the City's transit system.
    (A) decide
    (B) decided
    (C) deciding
    (D) decidedly

129. Although the environmental organization has a limited -------, it has managed to hold a number of informative workshops and discussion forums.
    (A) amount
    (B) fund
    (C) quantity
    (D) quality

130. ------- meet the increasing needs of tourists, a number of hotels should be renovated or newly built.
    (A) In order to
    (B) Just as
    (C) Only if
    (D) In addition to

## PART 6

**Directions:** Read the texts that follow. A word, phrase, or sentence is missing in parts of each text. Four answer choices for each question are given below the text. Select the best answer to complete the text. Then mark the letter (A), (B), (C), or (D) on your answer sheet.

**Questions 131-134** refer to the following article.

The Best Family Foundation offers free divorce workshops every Monday morning. Sign-ins for the workshops are Monday mornings at 10:00 am in The Best Family Foundation office. -------.
        **131.**

Note: Anyone who is wishing to start a divorce, a legal separation, or an annulment and is seeking assistance from the consultant must attend this workshop first.

You must also ------- the following:
        **132.**

* Please purchase a Divorce Packet from the Business Office for $10.00 ------- coming to the
                                                 **133.**
workshop. This packet includes all the forms you will need on the day of the workshop.

* Please bring a black ink pen. Pencils and blue pens are NOT -------.
                                                   **134.**

* There will be no translation service. If you are not fluent in English, you had better to bring your own translator.

* Children are not allowed to attend the workshop, but childcare service is available.

131. (A) Please take your seat in advance, in case of full reservation
    (B) Take part in the morning workshop, and listen to the lecture
    (C) Plan to spend the entire morning there, as the workshop lasts until 12:00 P.M
    (D) Go to the consultant to fill the form in

132. (A) do
    (B) did
    (C) done
    (D) doing

133. (A) after
    (B) before
    (C) during
    (D) with

134. (A) acceptable
    (B) responsible
    (C) dependable
    (D) feasible

GO ON TO THE NEXT PAGE

---

Courtney Saint
341 S. Bellefield Ave.
Pittsburgh, PA 15213

**OBJECTIVE**

A senior management position in which experience in sales and management can increase sales and profitability of major products. -------.
                                              **135.**

**SUMMARY OF SKILLS**

» Strong educational background and experience in marketing and sales
» Adaptability when working with diverse groups of people
» Capable of building and maintaining long lasting relationships with customers
» Ambitious and hard-working, with a commitment to excellence
» Willing to relocate or travel as -------
                            **136.**

**EMPLOYMENT EXPERIENCE**

June 2021 - Present

Sales Associate / Receptionist for Lisa's Hair and Tan, Pittsburgh, PA
» Sold hair care and tanning products on a daily basis
» Responsible ------- inventory control, ordering, and bookkeeping
              **137.**
» Utilized exceptional cash management techniques on a daily basis
» Made presentations for customers to promote tanning solution sales

August 2011 - May 2021

Sales Associate for Tracy's Wholesale Clubs, Pittsburgh, PA
» Assisted customers in making decisions by utilizing knowledge of products
» Consistently exceeded individual sales quota for each seven-day period by 30%
» Developed various promotional events to ------- more customers
                         **138.**
» Made presentations for customers and sold extended warranties on electronic products

References Available Upon Request

---

135. (A) In addition, I was regarded as the expert in the sales department
    (B) Moreover, I am good at working with diverse groups of people
    (C) Plus, I have already made many presentations for customers to promote tanning solution sales
    (D) Additionally, I have a strong educational background in marketing

136. (A) need
    (B) needed
    (C) needs
    (D) needing

137. (A) for
    (B) to
    (C) of
    (D) on

138. (A) attract
    (B) satisfy
    (C) impress
    (D) move

Questions 139-142 refer to the following notice.

---

**Cellular Phone Policy**

All employees are reminded to obtain approval from their manager prior to using personal cellular phones for business purposes. Personal cellular phone use for business should be limited to only necessary and immediate business needs. It is the responsibility of the managers to ------- the cellular phone usage of all employees.
**139.**

All employees who make business calls on their personal cellular phones will be reimbursed at a flat rate of $1.00 per minute regardless of the user's service plans.

-------. Requests should indicate Business calls on a personal cellular phone, number of
**140.**
minutes at $1.00/minute, and the dates the calls were made. All employees should retain documentation supporting any request for reimbursement but they do NOT need to attach such documentation for requests less than $100. Reimbursement requests for more than $100 will require ------- a log which identifies individual calls by number of minutes, an area
**141.**
code, and a phone number or a copy of the mobile phone bill. The mobile phone bill should identify the calls for which reimbursement is requested.

To keep processing and administration costs to a minimum, all employees are encouraged to accumulate at least $100 in business mobile phone charges before ------- requests for
**142.**
reimbursement, unless requests are combined with other reimbursement requests that exceed the $100 minimum.

---

**139.** (A) monitor
(B) control
(C) investigate
(D) hear

**140.** (A) An Expense Voucher should be repaid at a flat rate of $1.00 per minute
(B) An Expense Voucher should be submitted for mobile phone reimbursement
(C) An Expense Voucher should be confined within prompt business needs
(D) An Expense Voucher should be limited to another reimbursement request

**141.** (A) not
(B) neither
(C) not only
(D) either

**142.** (A) submit
(B) submits
(C) submitted
(D) submitting

GO ON TO THE NEXT PAGE

Jayson F. Murphy
414 North Central Avenue
Phoenix. Arizona 85012
(602) 375-2599


Dear Ms. Donnie Copper

This e-mail is to be sent in response to inquiries regarding the start date of the

development of our new pharmaceutical product. We are scheduled ------- the
**143.**

manufacturing process immediately after receiving the grant from the Municipal Wellbeing

Fund, which should occur by July 31st.

At the moment, the state is still processing our grant application. As you know, I applied for

this grant over two months ago and was told that the approval process would take only three

weeks. The state appears to have ------- my grant application since that time. -------.
**144.**                                                        **145.**

In the meantime, notify ------- employees in your departments that there will be an all day
**146.**
meeting on July 4 to remap our manufacturing schedule for the product.

Thank you for your patience and cooperation.

Jayson F. Murphy

---

**143.** (A) began
(B) begun
(C) beginning
(D) to begin

**144.** (A) displaced
(B) replaced
(C) misplaced
(D) placed

**145.** (A) The state government informed me of its approval before they sent us an e-mail on June 31st
(B) Today, we must process our grant application to the state before July 31st
(C) I should tell the state that it will take two weeks to process the approval request
(D) Fortunately, today the state controller assured me that we will receive approval by the end of the month

**146.** (A) all
(B) every
(C) each
(D) any

**Directions:** In this part you will read a selection of texts, such as magazine and newspaper articles, e-mails, and instant messages. Each text or set of texts is followed by several questions. Select the best answer for each question and mark the letter (A), (B), (C), or (D) on your answer sheet.

**Questions 147-148** refer to the following advertisement.

---

## *Great phone!*
## *Great deal!*

### *Find out what you can obtain from us and call now.*

§ **Free Headset!**

So you can receive and make calls without using your hands!

§ **Free delivery!**

Hey, our company will even pay the shipping costs. What a great deal!

§ **Great wireless plans as low as $29.99 a month**

You can make and receive a call across campus, across town or across the country.

§ **Free installation fee!**

You can install the wireless router for free.

§ **Easy 2-months trial!**

You can try it for up to 2 months at no cost! So if you're not completely satisfied, just return your equipment within the 2-months trial period.

**What are you waiting for?**

Call now toll-free 2-634-642-8744

Use promotion code 34655 for a discount!

HT&T's 2 months trial applies when you purchase a Digital multi-network phone and activate new service.

In order to receive a full refund, the phone must be in good condition. Return cancellation after the 2-months trial period will cause the imposition of a cancellation fee.

This offer is subject to change and will expire 12-31-24. This offer is only valid when you call the toll-free number. This offer may require credit approval.

---

**147.** Which of the following is NOT mentioned as an advantage of the promotion?

(A) The customers can try the product up to 2 months.

(B) When returning the phone, it must be in a good condition.

(C) The order must be placed on-line.

(D) The customers will receive a hands-free head-set.

**148.** When does this promotion plan end?

(A) In ten days

(B) At the end of the year 2024

(C) When the company gives out another notice

(D) It will be valid thru June 2024.

*GO ON TO THE NEXT PAGE*

Questions 149-150 refer to the following text message chain.

| Text Message | _ □ × |
|---|---|

| **Drew Sanders** 10:54 A.M. | Today I visited the restaurant, and they couldn't accommodate us because there was no record of our reservation. |
|---|---|
| **Malik Simmons** 10:56 A.M. | No way. Yesterday morning I called and got a confirmation. You should double check for the reservation. |
| **Drew Sanders** 10:59 A.M. | I already checked multiple times. Anyway, that's what they're telling me. We'll have to find somewhere else to go for dinner. |
| **Malik Simmons** 11:00 A.M. | Have the guests arrived yet? |
| **Drew Sanders** 11:01 A.M. | No, but I'm guessing that they'll be here any minute. Could you call some restaurants in the area and check if we can get a table? |
| **Malik Simmons** 11:03 A.M. | I see. Try to keep them entertained until I get there. I'm still about 30 minutes away. |
| **Drew Sanders** 11:05 A.M. | I'll do my best. But please hurry. |
| **Malik Simmons** 11:08 A.M. | Yes, I will. Sorry for being late. See you soon! |

Send

149. What is true about Mr. Drew Sanders?

(A) He is Ms. Malik Sanders' coworker.
(B) He didn't check his reservation.
(C) He didn't talk to his customer.
(D) He is working at the restaurant.

150. At 10:56 A.M., what does Ms. Malik Simmons mean when she writes, "No way"?

(A) She is unsure that the restaurant lost her reservation.
(B) She didn't remember to call the restaurant.
(C) She mistook the reservation for the final decision.
(D) She didn't know that the reservation was canceled.

FROM: trademarket@freetrade.com

SENT: July 3, 2023

TO: mrnorman@english.com

Subject: Make your business better with us!

Dear Mr. Norman,

Freetrade.com offers immediate worldwide exposure as well as safe, easy access to importers and exporters, sales agents, retail dealers, wholesalers, and service providers for small and medium-sized companies associated with business trade.

Expose your company's name to the world. Worldwide exposure is necessary in today's terribly competitive import-export market. List your firm on the Freetrade.com marketplace and benefit from our web trade services.
Contact http://www.freetrade.com today to list your firm.
Our membership is always available to you at no cost.

Dallas, Texas

Phone: 34-553-3571-664~6,

Fax: 44-5352-332-644

Best regards,

Russel L. Stevens

151. Why did Russel L. Stevens send this e-mail?

(A) To supply price and policy information of Freetrade.com
(B) To explain the worldwide issues
(C) To make companies join Freetrade.com
(D) To cancel the reservation

152. Which of the following doesn't Freetrade.com offer business advertisement to?

(A) Manufacturers
(B) Retail dealers
(C) Wholesalers
(D) Importers

*GO ON TO THE NEXT PAGE*

////////////////////////////////////////////////////////////////////////////////

Elwood Weisman
Super Credit Card
253 King Street, Chicago, IL 10412
Telephone : 323-422-6844
Fax : 323-422-5933

Dear Ms. Lozano,
I am happy to notify you that our company has approved a charge account in your name. We welcome you as a new client and wish that you enjoy the convenience of your charge account.

A credit limit of $10,000 has been established on your account. If you want to raise the credit limit, please make a phone call or visit our credit office. Then, we should expedite our handling of your request.

Your card and our pamphlet has been enclosed in the mail which explains our billing procedure, how to use your credit card, and additional information we believe you will find useful. If you wish to know further details, please visit our web site. www. supercard.com

Thank you again for choosing our card company.

Sincerely,
Elwood Weisman

////////////////////////////////////////////////////////////////////////////////

153. What is the purpose of this letter?

    (A) To inform that they have sent the card

    (B) To announce that their proposal has been denied

    (C) To show that she needs to register the credit card

    (D) To notify that there is no credit limit

154. What has the company enclosed?

    (A) A list of customer numbers

    (B) A note

    (C) A brochure

    (D) A business card

## Notice to Our Clients!

Last updated: December 22, 2022

Bookstore.com knows that you care how your data and personal information is used and shared, and we thank you for trusting that we will deal with it carefully and wisely. You are accepting the regulation described in this Privacy Policy Notice by visiting Bookstore.com.

*What personal data and information about clients does Bookstore.com gather?*

The information we learn from clients helps us personalize and continually improve your shopping experience at Bookstore.com. Here are the types of data and information we collect :

*Information You Give Us :*

We obtain and store any data and information you enter on our web page or give us in any other way. Check examples of what we gather. You can choose not to give certain data and information, but then you might not be able to take advantage of our numerous features. We make use of the information that you give us for such purposes as easily communicating with you, responding to your inquiries, customizing your future shopping for you, and improving our store environment.

*E-mail Communications :*

In order to help us make e-mails more interesting and useful, we receive a confirmation when you open e-mail from Bookstore.com if your computer supports such capabilities. Also, We compare our client list to lists gained from other firms, in an effort to avoid sending needless messages and information to our clients. If you do not hope to receive mail or e-mail from our company, please change your Client Communication Preferences. If you do not change your communication preferences, our mailing system continue sending mail or e-mail to you.

*Information from Other Sources :*

We might receive data and information related to you from other sources and add it to our customer account information.

---

**155.** What is this notice about?

(A) Privacy policy of Bookstore.com
(B) Newly revised return policy
(C) One to one customer service
(D) Special order service for out-of-stock products

**156.** What is NOT true about the notice?

(A) Bookstore.com keeps personal information of customers for a certain period.
(B) Customers can refuse to provide certain information.
(C) Bookstore.com is gathering information of customers in many ways.
(D) Bookstore.com compares its customer list to ones from other companies.

**157.** According to the notice, what is the purpose of Bookstore.com for gathering customers' personal information?

(A) To figure out its sales amount for the yearly report.
(B) To personalize and continually improve customers' shopping experience
(C) To arrange information for subcontractors
(D) To attract shoppers with its vast database to Bookstore.com

*GO ON TO THE NEXT PAGE* ➡

Questions 158-160 refer to the following memo.

Dear precious employees,

--- [1] ---. This year has been a difficult time for FLK, Inc. Everybody knows that the cancellation of our four contracts with the France Air Force due to the reduction in defence expenses, hurt us considerably.

--- [2] ---. The choices which we were faced with was whether to let some of our employees go, or to find all other possible methods of cutting back cost while leaving everyone's jobs intact. We chose the latter. Unfortunately, one of the regulations which we were forced to revise this year, was our annual year-end bonus for all employees, because this year's revenue has decreased significantly from last year's.

--- [3] ---. For the second time, since 1980's, we will be unable to show our appreciation for you in this special manner for your hard work, excellent performance, and faithfulness. We are all hoping that 2008 will be a successful year and that we will be able to restore our traditional year-end bonus regulation. --- [4] ---.

**158.** Where would this memo most likely be found?

(A) In a newspaper
(B) In a vice-president's office
(C) On a company bulletin board
(D) In an annual report.

**159.** Why has the company been in financial difficulty this year?

(A) Cancellation of contracts
(B) Provided excessive bonuses to the employees
(C) Decline of the company's stock
(D) Unfair dismissal of employees

**160.** In which of the positions marked [1], [2], [3] and [4] does the following sentence best belong?

"In August, we made a serious decision."

(A) [1]
(B) [2]
(C) [3]
(D) [4]

**Spectacular Holiday Clothing Show**

**Hours**: Daily 11 A.M.-7 P.M. / Sun 11 A.M.-6 P.M.

Spectacular Holiday Clothing Show will be held by the New York Vintage. More than 30 top dealers will attend to help you to fill your holiday stockings with care. Show highlights include:

- **Long Fur Jackets**: cozy and warm like a puppy and very portable
- **Lingerie Style**: the latest boudoir-inspired styles let you be sophisticated and sexy.
- **Glamorous Gloves**: the most important accessory for ladies

**MHSALE Members**: Save $15 off the regular admission fee of $30. Click here to buy tickets online now or print and bring this web page to receive a special discount. Don't miss this great 3-day vintage fashion show. All the events will take place at the Bella Building

**Payment Type**: Cash/ VISA/ MC/ AMEX/

**Address**: 481 Rubble Street, (The Bella Building), Manhattan, MH 21442, (553) 503-3324

161. According to the advertisement, what are the most important decorations for women?

(A) Fur jackets
(B) Gloves
(C) Boudoir
(D) Holiday stockings

162. How much of a discount can a MHSALE member receive on the admission to this show?

(A) 15%
(B) 30%
(C) 45%
(D) 50%

163. Where will this show take place?

(A) In an grape orchard
(B) In a stadium
(C) In a park
(D) In a building

GO ON TO THE NEXT PAGE

**Questions 164-167** refer to the following online chat discussion.

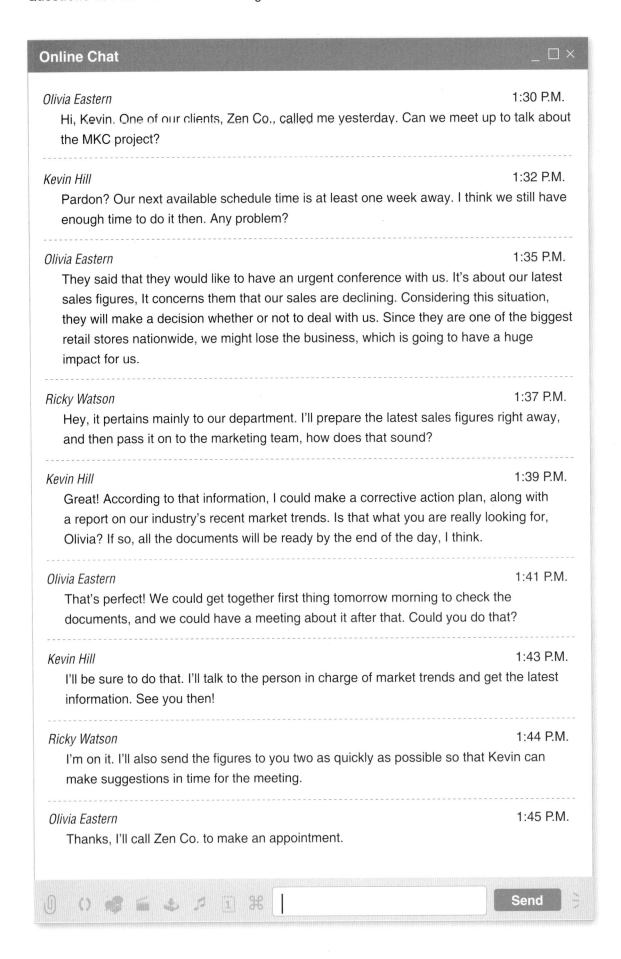

**Online Chat**     _ □ ×

| | |
|---|---|
| *Olivia Eastern* | 1:30 P.M. |

Hi, Kevin. One of our clients, Zen Co., called me yesterday. Can we meet up to talk about the MKC project?

| | |
|---|---|
| *Kevin Hill* | 1:32 P.M. |

Pardon? Our next available schedule time is at least one week away. I think we still have enough time to do it then. Any problem?

| | |
|---|---|
| *Olivia Eastern* | 1:35 P.M. |

They said that they would like to have an urgent conference with us. It's about our latest sales figures, It concerns them that our sales are declining. Considering this situation, they will make a decision whether or not to deal with us. Since they are one of the biggest retail stores nationwide, we might lose the business, which is going to have a huge impact for us.

| | |
|---|---|
| *Ricky Watson* | 1:37 P.M. |

Hey, it pertains mainly to our department. I'll prepare the latest sales figures right away, and then pass it on to the marketing team, how does that sound?

| | |
|---|---|
| *Kevin Hill* | 1:39 P.M. |

Great! According to that information, I could make a corrective action plan, along with a report on our industry's recent market trends. Is that what you are really looking for, Olivia? If so, all the documents will be ready by the end of the day, I think.

| | |
|---|---|
| *Olivia Eastern* | 1:41 P.M. |

That's perfect! We could get together first thing tomorrow morning to check the documents, and we could have a meeting about it after that. Could you do that?

| | |
|---|---|
| *Kevin Hill* | 1:43 P.M. |

I'll be sure to do that. I'll talk to the person in charge of market trends and get the latest information. See you then!

| | |
|---|---|
| *Ricky Watson* | 1:44 P.M. |

I'm on it. I'll also send the figures to you two as quickly as possible so that Kevin can make suggestions in time for the meeting.

| | |
|---|---|
| *Olivia Eastern* | 1:45 P.M. |

Thanks, I'll call Zen Co. to make an appointment.

Send

**164.** What is Zen Co. worried about?

(A) Ms. Olivia Eastern and Mr. Kevin Hill can't meet.
(B) The low sales of Olivia's company.
(C) Mr. Kevin Hill is lack of time.
(D) The urgent meeting won't be held.

**165.** What is indicated about Mr. Ricky Watson?

(A) He works in the sales department.
(B) He used to manage a retail shop.
(C) He wrote the latest monthly report.
(D) He lost his document recently.

**166.** At 1:43 P.M., what does Mr. Kevin Hill mean when he writes "I'll be sure to do that"?

(A) He will contact Ms. Olivia Eastern.
(B) He will input some data into his computer.
(C) He will collect the necessary information.
(D) He will see Mr. Ricky Watson.

**167.** What will do Ms. Olivia Eastern next?

(A) Suggest her idea to Mr. Kevin Hill
(B) Send the sales figures too fast
(C) Encourage Mr. Ricky Watson to check the data
(D) Contact Zen Co.

*GO ON TO THE NEXT PAGE*

Hiking is a great form of exercise that almost anybody can take part in. All you really need is a love for the outdoors. While the more experienced people can go straight up a mountain, beginners can continue easy flat walking exercises. Almost every park in the state has trails that range from easy exercise to challenging exercise, at little or no cost.

**Starting Out**

Find a nature preserve or a park. If you have any friends or family members, bring them along! Hiking is an excellent group activity, but numerous people like to hike on their own. Be sure you tell someone where you're going and when you intend to return if you are solo. It is a must in case that you get lost or injured.

**Target areas**

It is an great endurance-building aerobic exercise and is the best way to burn calories. You just need to maintain a steady pace. Also, it will help build muscle strength, particularly in your hamstrings, calves, gluteus muscles, and quadriceps. Because it is a weight-bearing activity, it will help make your bones strong. And if you carry a backpack, the extra weight of the backpack will help you burn even more calories and lose weight. You don't have to carry the weight to burn more calories if you can't handle it. Be responsible.

**The Cool-Down and Warm-Up**

Begin at a slow pace. If the trail begins roughly, you may first need to take a few minutes to walk around on easier terrain. It takes 10 to 15 minutes to warm up your muscles, get your heart rate up and break a sweat (a sign that you're ready to proceed).

Cool down by slowing to a walk for five to ten minutes to help your heart rate drop slowly before the end of your exercise.

Be sure to stretch the major muscle groups after you warm up to prevent your body from getting injured and again after exercising to promote flexibility and prevent soreness.

168. What is this information about?

(A) Cycling
(B) Running
(C) Hiking
(D) Diving

169. What can be recommended for beginners?

(A) Going straight up the mountain
(B) Beginning walking on flat tracks
(C) Telling others how long you're going to exercise
(D) Building up muscles

170. What should you do after you're done with this exercise?

(A) Take a deep breath
(B) Stretch your body
(C) Drink a glass of water
(D) Time your heartbeat

171. Which of the following is NOT good way for hiking?

(A) Carrying a backpack while hiking
(B) Gradually walking at a fast pace
(C) Finding any park and practicing walking
(D) Walking a few minutes and timing your heartbeat before hiking

GO ON TO THE NEXT PAGE

We are informing you of the incident which occurred at the following location:

Lake Worth Apartment Complex
Naples FL

This incident has been reported to the proper law enforcement agency, and to our knowledge, the criminal responsible for this incident has not been arrested or identified.

The report as given to us by law enforcement states the following:

In the last two weeks the Maryland Heights and Creve Coeur Police have had complaints of a "PEEPING TOM" in apartment communities. The last report was at Lake Worth Apartment Complex. The following is a description of the "PEEPING TOM":
Black male, approximately 5'7" tall, Middle aged, black hair, tan complexion, and the suspect was last seen wearing jogging shorts without a shirt. --- [1] ---.

We urge that you should take precautions for your protection. While nothing can guarantee that you do not become the victim of a crime, there are a few steps that can reduce your risk of becoming a victim. --- [2] ---.

- When entering the apartment complex, if you notice a suspicious man, drive to the nearest phone and call the police. Thereafter, notify the apartment complex office as soon as possible.

- While at home in your apartment, keep all doors and windows locked.

- Always ask for identification before allowing anyone into your apartment and Never open your apartment door for strange man.

- If you feel threatened at any time , notify the police by calling 112.

- If you should become a victim of crime, report it immediately to the Police Department and then notify the apartment complex office.

--- [3] ---. Remember we care about your safety, but crimes can occur at any time and any place. We do not want you to become a victim, so please always do the reasonable personal security steps. --- [4] ---.

The following phone numbers are provided for your convenience:

Police Department: (413) 787-5462
Management Office: (413) 787-2020

Brian O'neil

Community Manager

172. What would be the best title for this notice?

(A) Peeping person
(B) Crime Alert Notice
(C) Job Openings
(D) Theft report

173. Which of the following crimes did the suspect commit?

(A) Theft
(B) Looking secretly at other people
(C) Arson
(D) Beating the pedestrians

174. How was the suspect described?

(A) White male
(B) Bald
(C) Tanned skin
(D) Young

175. In which of the positions marked [1], [2], [3] and [4] does the following sentence best belong?

"We are hoping for the cooperation of everybody to aid in the arrest of the criminal in our city."

(A) [1]
(B) [2]
(C) [3]
(D) [4]

*GO ON TO THE NEXT PAGE*

**Questions 176-180** refer to the following e-mail and attachment.

| To | Joshua Morris |
|---|---|
| From | Dwain Anderson, Human Resources |

Dear Mr. Morris,

Thank you for writing back to me so soon. The starting date that you indicated is satisfactory to our needs. As one of our new recruits, you will be required to attend a group orientation, the schedule of which is attached to this e-mail; this will be your first of four days of training. You have been placed into Group A.

You will be issued an employee manual by our senior training supervisor following the orientation speech by the CEO. Familiarize yourself with all company guidelines by the end of the third day of training, as there will be a test on the final day. Questions regarding the handbook should be addressed to your group leader.

As we discussed, there will be a paid probationary period of one month, after which you will be working solely on commission and will be required to meet a weekly sales quota. In the meantime, let me know if you need anything else to be clarified about the position.

Best regards,
Dwain Anderson

### Victoria Corporation

\* Orientation Schedule

| 9:00 am | Kory Gonzales<br>- Orientation address : The past, present, and future of Victoria Corporation, and corporate mission overview. |
|---|---|
| 11:00 am | Michael Collins<br>- Presentation of company policy and employee handbooks.<br>- Introduction of training-group leaders. |
| 12:00 pm | Lunch break |
| 1:00 pm-6:00 pm | Group training |

\* Training-Group Leaders

Group A : Frank williams, Sales and Marketing Training Supervisor
Group B : Lionel Blackstone, Data Entry Training Supervisor
Group C : Hannah Evans, Chief of Security and Security Training Supervisor

176. Which of the following best describes the e-mail?

(A) A response to a job advertisement
(B) An offer of employment to a candidate
(C) An invitation to a corporate seminar
(D) An outline of basic company policies

177. Who is Kory Gonzales?

(A) The human resources manager
(B) The CEO of Victoria Corporation
(C) The senior training supervisor
(D) The founder of the company

178. Who should Mr. Morris ask about the content of the handbook?

(A) Frank Williams
(B) Michael Collins
(C) Dwain Anderson
(D) Lionel Blackstone

179. What can be inferred about the recipient of the e-mail?

(A) He will not start working until next month.
(B) He will be hired as a sales representative.
(C) He will work in the personnel department.
(D) He will be issued a security ID badge.

180. What will happen on the final day of the orientation?

(A) Mr. Morris will start earning a commission.
(B) Trainees will be asked to take a policy exam.
(C) Kory Gonzales will make a speech.
(D) The company guidelines will be revised.

GO ON TO THE NEXT PAGE

To whom it may concern,

I am writing to tell you how much I was disappointed with your restaurant. On September 25, I ate lunch at The Capriatti. I have eaten there many times before with no problems. However, when I arrived at noon on that day, I sat alone with no service for almost 20 minutes until a waitress, Mary Collins, finally came to take my order. She also forgot to refill my water glass once I had finished it. This normally wouldn't bother me, but it was a very hot day and I was quite thirsty. Finally, once the food arrived at 12:40 I realized that instead of the salad I had requested with my sandwich, I had been served fries, and had to wait even longer for my salad to come. Needless to say, I was late to a conference call scheduled at 1:30. I generally enjoy eating at The Capriatti and the service is usually very good, but this time I was disappointed in my experience there.

Sincerely,
Rene Gibson

Dear Ms. Rene Gibson,

I am deeply sorry about what you recently experienced at The Capriatti. I must admit that September 25 was very hectic due to the convention at the Hilton Hotel across the street. However, this is no excuse for what happened to you. I have talked to Mary on the importance of attending to every customer in a timely manner. I will also make sure that in the future, when I know we are likely to be so busy, backup staff will be on the call to handle the extra work. Enclosed with this letter is a gift certificate for one complimentary lunch at The Capriatti as compensation for your recent unpleasant experience. I apologize for all the inconvenience you experienced due to our negligence and sincerely hope you will continue your patronage of our restaurant.

Sincerely,
Kendrick White, manager

181. Which of the following did the customer NOT complain about in the letter?

(A) The slow service
(B) The poor quality of the food
(C) The mistake with her order
(D) The inattentive waitress

182. What happened to Ms. Rene Gibson because of the delay?

(A) She was unable to finish eating.
(B) She was late for a lunch meeting.
(C) She missed a telephone call.
(D) She had to postpone her convention speech.

183. At what time did Ms. Rene Gibson order her meal?

(A) 12:00
(B) 12:20
(C) 12:40
(D) 1:30

184. What has the manager done to compensate for Ms. Rene Gibson's complaints?

(A) Offered her a free meal
(B) Dismissed Mary from her job
(C) Hired a new chef
(D) Asked the waitress to apologize

185. What was the likely cause of the problem?

(A) The waitress was new.
(B) The restaurant was full.
(C) The cook was inexperienced.
(D) The customer was impatient.

GO ON TO THE NEXT PAGE

**Questions 186-190** refer to the following e-mail, table and text message.

| | |
|---|---|
| *To* | Hilton Arnold <hiltonaaa@ringusa.net> |
| *From* | Donovan Oliver <doliver100@ringusa.net> |
| *Date* | 10 August 2024 |
| *Subject* | Re : New dialing rate from the competition |

Dear Ms. Hilton Arnold,

As you know, TeleGS is cutting its prices. Here you can see the chart of the pricing options they're planning to offer. We have always undercut the prices. If we don't change our rate structure, we will be at a disadvantage compared to our competitors during the first time. We need to respond with a price-cut of our own, but merely matching their rates won't work. They have cut rates on the traditional time and distance model as low as they can go.

We need a new business model! I have been asked to gather ideas. Should we go to a fixed monthly fee? Should individual calls be charged a unit charge regardless of the time or distance? New technologies are making the old system of hours and distances obsolete, but the direction we go is still unclear. Get back to me, and I'll lay out all the ideas I receive.

Best regards,

Donovan Oliver
General Manager
Ring USA Ltd.

## Rate Table of TeleGS

| | Time | Distance | Rates |
|---|---|---|---|
| **Regular** | 09:00 A.M. ~ 18:00 P.M. Monday to Friday | Under 100 km | $0.40 |
| | | 100 km ~ 500 km | $0.55 |
| | | 500 km ~ 1000 km | $0.70 |
| | | Over 1000 km | $0.80 |
| **Reduced** | 06:00 A.M. ~ 09:00 A.M. & 18:00 P.M. ~ 21:00 P.M. Monday to Friday 06:00 A.M. ~ 21:00 P.M. Only Saturday and Sunday | Under 100 km | $0.35 |
| | | 100 km ~ 500 km | $0.40 |
| | | 500 km ~ 1000 km | $0.50 |
| | | Over 1000 km | $0.60 |
| **Super Reduced** | 21:00 P.M. ~ 06:00 A.M. Daily | Under 100 km | $0.25 |
| | | 100 km ~ 500 km | $0.30 |
| | | 500 km ~ 1000 km | $0.35 |
| | | Over 1000 km | $0.40 |

Every three minutes

To : Donovan Oliver

My idea isn't like either of those two ideas. Let's offer unlimited nationwide calling to pre-determined frequent contacts. We could suggest a sliding scale of, say, five dollars a month to the first number. Then, we'd charge a lower additional fee for the second, third and fourth number. These could be cell phones, land lines and Wi-fi. Many people have friends and family who live far away and would save money if they call frequently. I know there will be a lot of different ideas, but I think this is the one our clients will understand and want.

From : Hilton Arnold

**186.** What does Mr. Donovan Oliver ask Ms. Hilton Arnold to do?

(A) To establish client target
(B) To invent a method to stay competitive
(C) To examine the price of rival companies
(D) To collect all ideas about our prices

**187.** In the e-mail, the word "obsolete", line 3, paragraph 2, is closest in meaning to

(A) outdated
(B) renewed
(C) lengthy
(D) brief

**188.** How long is Reduce service on Saturday and Sunday?

(A) 15 hours
(B) 24 hours
(C) 30 hours
(D) 48 hours

**189.** What can be inferred about Ms. Hilton Arnold?

(A) She would offer free local calls.
(B) She would give many customers the selling phone time by the hour.
(C) She would encourage people to call at the cheapest rate.
(D) She would suggest unlimited calling to a distance phone.

**190.** Which of the following is NOT included in TeleGS service?

(A) Mobile phone
(B) Land line
(C) Wi-fi
(D) Wire internet

*GO ON TO THE NEXT PAGE*

**Questions 191-195** refer to the following schedule and two e-mails.

## 15th Quarterly Small Business Conference Schedule

| Time | Topic |
|---|---|
| 09:30 A.M. | Opening Address<br>Mr. Otis Bell - Local Chamber of Commerce |
| 10:00 A.M. | Changes to Taxation Law<br>Mr. Kurt Morgan - Morgan Chartered Accountants |
| 10:30 A.M. | Expansion Strategies<br>Ms. Graham Cook - Goldstar Consulting Co. |
| 11:00 A.M. | Break |
| 11:20 A.M. | Community Liaison and Integration<br>Dr. Jessie Reed - Columbia University |
| 11:40 A.M. | Human Resources Management<br>Mr. Troy Stewart - E & F Ltd. |
| 12:00 P.M. | Lunch |
| 13:00 P.M. | Cash flow and Financial Planning<br>Ms. Lisa Edward - Atlantic Banking Corporation |
| 14:00 P.M. | Open Forum (Questions and Answers) |
| 15:00 P.M. | Closing Address<br>Mr. Otis Bell - Local Chamber of Commerce |

To : Mr. Otis Bell
From : Jessie Reed
Date : November 20
Sub : Small Business Conference

I appreciate your invitation for me to speak at the 15th Quarterly Small Business Conference. It was a great honor to participate as a guest speaker at the event last year, and I really want to go this conference. Unfortunately, January is an extremely busy month for me this year as I am required to finalize a new program for implementation in March. As much as I would like to attend, circumstances prevent me from doing so. I sincerely apologize for any inconveniences I have caused, and wish you success for this year's conference.

Yours sincerely,
Jessie Reed

| To | Mr. Teddy Hackman |
|----|-------------------|
| From | Mr. Otis Bell |
| Date | February 5 |
| Subject | Re : Small Business Conference |

Dear Mr. Teddy Hackman,

I am very sorry for late reply to your letter, because I had been busy trying to finalize annual financial reports. Firstly, I would like to thank you for filling in to speak at such short notice at the Small Business Conference. Your exceptional knowledge of the latest industry developments and insight into future trends made your presentation stand out amongst the others. I have received nothing but positive feedback, with particular interest in the online freight tracking system your company recently developed.

Again, thank you for your assistance and I wish you continuing success and prosperity in the year ahead.

Best regards,

Otis Bell

191. According to the schedule, who spoke about mergers and acquisitions of other companies?

(A) Mr. Otis Bell
(B) Mr. Kurt Morgan
(C) Ms. Graham Cook
(D) Dr. Jessie Reed

192. What is the purpose of the first e-mail?

(A) To welcome a coworker
(B) To accept the proposal
(C) To decline an offer
(D) To ask about a schedule

193. What is true about Ms. Jessie Reed?

(A) She invited Mr. Otis Bell to attend in the conference.
(B) She had little work to do in January.
(C) She has to make a new program in March.
(D) She has addressed at the conference before.

194. Why is Mr. Otis Bell's e-mail to Mr. Teddy Hackman delayed?

(A) Because Mr. Otis Bell apologizes to Mr. Teddy Hackman
(B) Because Mr. Otis Bell has to complete his financial report
(C) Because Mr. Otis Bell welcomes Mr. Teddy Hackman's invitation
(D) Because Mr. Otis Bell received the positive reply

195. What will Mr. Teddy Hackman's presentation most likely be about?

(A) Shipping and handling
(B) Quality control
(C) Online banking system
(D) Funding method

*GO ON TO THE NEXT PAGE*

## Top Games of the Year, 2024

| Rank | Title | Developer | Genre |
|------|-------|-----------|-------|
| 1 | Minecraft Pocket Edition | Mojang | Sandbox, Survival |
| 2 | Words with Friends | Zynga | Education |
| 3 | Solitaire | Silver Games | Board & Card |
| 4 | Geometry Dash | RobTop Games | Arcade |
| 5 | Massed NFL Mobile | EA SPORTS | Sports |
| 6 | Temple Run 2 | Imangi Studios | Arcade |

**E-Mail** _ □ ×

| To | Danford Forest | Cc Bcc |
|----|----------------|--------|
| From | Jeniffer Hart | |
| Date | 16, February, Friday | |

| Subject | Re : Games list |
|---------|-----------------|

Dear Mr. Danford Forest,
I just got the short list of the names of last year's top five best-selling mobile games. According to the sales, in order, there are : Minecraft: Pocket Edition, Words with Friends, Solitaire, Geometry Dash, and Temple Run 2.

What I need you and your team to do is to check the software developer company and genre for each game, and then rank them depending on your research on consumer reports. For now, all I need is your ranking and any points you think are important. You can give me the full details later when we draft a report for the committee for game control.

I am looking forward to your report.

Best regards,
Jeniffer Hart

Send

Jeniffer Hart

Thanks for your patience. I had wanted to get this to you sooner, but we came across a couple of surprises while researching the games. first, you will notice an extra item. While we were researching EA SPORTS, we noticed they came out with a new game whose reviews were better than the one by Imangi Studios. We think it's rare for a Sports-related game to get such good reviews.

We'd like your opinion on what to do with the list. Does it need to be five items, or can it be more?

Looking forward to your reply.

Danford Forest

196. Which of the following are the game genre same?

(A) Temple Run 2 and Minecraft Pocket Edition
(B) Geometry Dash and Word with Friend
(C) Solitaire and Massed NFL Mobile
(D) Geometry Dash and Temple Run 2

197. Where do Mr. Danford Forest and Ms. Jeniffer Hart work for?

(A) A computer shop
(B) A software marketing company
(C) An educational institute
(D) A stationary store

198. What does the chart say about Minecraft Pocket Edition?

(A) It was ranked fast.
(B) It was discussed in a conference.
(C) It was seen in a consumer report.
(D) It was the top game of the year.

199. What does Mr. Danford Forest ask Ms. Jeniffer Hart?

(A) If there can be more than five items on the list
(B) Develop some games
(C) Examine some computers
(D) Report the rank to some consumers

200. What game does Mr. Danford Forest add to the list?

(A) Words with Friends
(B) Solitaire
(C) Geometry Dash
(D) Massed NFL Mobile

**Stop! This is the end of the test. If you finish before time is called, you may go back to Parts 5, 6, and 7 and check your work.**

GO ON TO THE NEXT PAGE

## 퀵 토익 실전모의고사 SET #2 정답

* 환산 점수는 정답 및 해설에서 확인하세요.

| | 응시일 | TEST 소요시간 | 맞은 개수 | 환산 점수 |
|---|---|---|---|---|
| LC | ___월 ___일 | _____ 분 | _____ 개 | _____ 점 |
| RC | | _____ 분 | _____ 개 | _____ 점 |

| PART 1 | PART 2 | PART 3 | | PART 4 | PART 5 | PART 6 | PART 7 | | |
|---|---|---|---|---|---|---|---|---|---|
| 1 (B) | 7 (B) | 32 (A) | 62 (B) | 71 (D) | 101 (B) | 131 (C) | 147 (D) | 176 (C) | 186 (B) |
| 2 (D) | 8 (A) | 33 (C) | 63 (D) | 72 (C) | 102 (B) | 132 (A) | 148 (A) | 177 (B) | 187 (A) |
| 3 (C) | 9 (B) | 34 (A) | 64 (B) | 73 (A) | 103 (C) | 133 (B) | 149 (A) | 178 (A) | 188 (C) |
| 4 (A) | 10 (A) | 35 (B) | 65 (C) | 74 (C) | 104 (D) | 134 (A) | 150 (A) | 179 (B) | 189 (D) |
| 5 (A) | 11 (C) | 36 (A) | 66 (C) | 75 (D) | 105 (C) | 135 (D) | 151 (C) | 180 (B) | 190 (D) |
| 6 (B) | 12 (B) | 37 (B) | 67 (A) | 76 (D) | 106 (C) | 136 (B) | 152 (A) | 181 (B) | 191 (C) |
| | 13 (A) | 38 (C) | 68 (C) | 77 (B) | 107 (C) | 137 (A) | 153 (A) | 182 (C) | 192 (C) |
| | 14 (C) | 39 (A) | 69 (B) | 78 (C) | 108 (A) | 138 (A) | 154 (C) | 183 (B) | 193 (D) |
| | 15 (A) | 40 (C) | 70 (C) | 79 (D) | 109 (A) | 139 (A) | 155 (A) | 184 (A) | 194 (B) |
| | 16 (C) | 41 (B) | | 80 (B) | 110 (C) | 140 (B) | 156 (A) | 185 (B) | 195 (A) |
| | 17 (B) | 42 (A) | | 81 (A) | 111 (C) | 141 (D) | 157 (B) | | 196 (D) |
| | 18 (C) | 43 (D) | | 82 (D) | 112 (D) | 142 (D) | 158 (C) | | 197 (B) |
| | 19 (B) | 44 (B) | | 83 (A) | 113 (C) | 143 (D) | 159 (A) | | 198 (D) |
| | 20 (B) | 45 (A) | | 84 (B) | 114 (B) | 144 (C) | 160 (B) | | 199 (A) |
| | 21 (C) | 46 (D) | | 85 (A) | 115 (D) | 145 (D) | 161 (B) | | 200 (D) |
| | 22 (C) | 47 (D) | | 86 (B) | 116 (B) | 146 (A) | 162 (D) | | |
| | 23 (B) | 48 (B) | | 87 (A) | 117 (A) | | 163 (D) | | |
| | 24 (B) | 49 (D) | | 88 (D) | 118 (C) | | 164 (B) | | |
| | 25 (B) | 50 (C) | | 89 (C) | 119 (B) | | 165 (A) | | |
| | 26 (A) | 51 (B) | | 90 (D) | 120 (A) | | 166 (C) | | |
| | 27 (C) | 52 (A) | | 91 (B) | 121 (D) | | 167 (D) | | |
| | 28 (A) | 53 (C) | | 92 (D) | 122 (B) | | 168 (C) | | |
| | 29 (C) | 54 (C) | | 93 (A) | 123 (D) | | 169 (B) | | |
| | 30 (A) | 55 (A) | | 94 (B) | 124 (C) | | 170 (B) | | |
| | 31 (C) | 56 (C) | | 95 (C) | 125 (D) | | 171 (D) | | |
| | | 57 (A) | | 96 (B) | 126 (B) | | 172 (B) | | |
| | | 58 (D) | | 97 (B) | 127 (C) | | 173 (B) | | |
| | | 59 (C) | | 98 (A) | 128 (D) | | 174 (C) | | |
| | | 60 (D) | | 99 (B) | 129 (B) | | 175 (D) | | |
| | | 61 (B) | | 100 (A) | 130 (A) | | | | |

# 퀵
# 토익
## 실전모의고사

SET #3

LC 음원

채점 &
정답 및 해설

지금부터 Actual Test를 진행합니다.
실제 시험과 동일한 방식으로 진행됨을 말씀드리며,
LC 음원은 QR코드로 청취할 수 있습니다.

준비되면 바로 시작하세요!

## LISTENING TEST

In the Listening test, you will be asked to demonstrate how well you understand spoken English. The entire Listening test will last approximately 45 minutes. There are four parts, and directions are given for each part. You must mark your answers on the separate answer sheet. Do not write your answers in your test book.

## PART 1

**Directions:** For each question in this part, you will hear four statements about a picture in your test book. When you hear the statements, you must select the one statement that best describes what you see in the picture. Then find the number of the question on your answer sheet and mark your answer. The statements will not be printed in your test book and will be spoken only one time.

Statment (A), "Some people are paddling through the water," is the best description of the picture, so you should select answer (A) and mark it on your answer sheet.

**1.**

**2.**

*GO ON TO THE NEXT PAGE* ➡

**3.**

**4.**

**5.**

**6.**

*GO ON TO THE NEXT PAGE* ➤

## PART 2

**Directions:** You will hear a question or statement and three responses spoken in English. They will not be printed in your test book and will be spoken only one time. Select the best response to the question or statement and mark the letter (A), (B), or (C) on your answer sheet.

7. Mark your answer on your answer sheet.

8. Mark your answer on your answer sheet.

9. Mark your answer on your answer sheet.

10. Mark your answer on your answer sheet.

11. Mark your answer on your answer sheet.

12. Mark your answer on your answer sheet.

13. Mark your answer on your answer sheet.

14. Mark your answer on your answer sheet.

15. Mark your answer on your answer sheet.

16. Mark your answer on your answer sheet.

17. Mark your answer on your answer sheet.

18. Mark your answer on your answer sheet.

19. Mark your answer on your answer sheet.

20. Mark your answer on your answer sheet.

21. Mark your answer on your answer sheet.

22. Mark your answer on your answer sheet.

23. Mark your answer on your answer sheet.

24. Mark your answer on your answer sheet.

25. Mark your answer on your answer sheet.

26. Mark your answer on your answer sheet.

27. Mark your answer on your answer sheet.

28. Mark your answer on your answer sheet.

29. Mark your answer on your answer sheet.

30. Mark your answer on your answer sheet.

31. Mark your answer on your answer sheet.

## PART 3

**Directions:** You will hear some conversations between two or more people. You will be asked to answer three questions about what the speakers say in each conversation. Select the best response to each question and mark the letter (A), (B), (C), or (D) on your answer sheet. The conversations will not be printed in your test book and will be spoken only one time.

32. Why is the woman calling the man?
    (A) To announce the advertising campaign
    (B) To notify the exchange of the agenda
    (C) To work at 25th streets branch
    (D) To remind him of the meeting

33. What does the man offer to do?
    (A) To use her tablet computer
    (B) To participate on the telephone
    (C) To receive the result of a meeting
    (D) To see the participants afterwards

34. What does the woman request the man do?
    (A) To send a document
    (B) To print his report
    (C) To find his seat
    (D) To request his budget from the firm

35. What problem does the man mention?
    (A) Negative view about his restaurant
    (B) His decreased business
    (C) The improper location of the restaurant
    (D) Increased waiting time

36. What solution does the woman propose?
    (A) Exchanging the seat locations
    (B) Relocating the cafeteria
    (C) Using the new marketing project
    (D) Additional seating

37. What does the man say he will do?
    (A) Use the company for renovation.
    (B) Consult the business owner.
    (C) Call the other restaurant.
    (D) Put more tables by the window.

38. What is the conversation mainly about?
    (A) The woman's hotel
    (B) The man's mission
    (C) The major attraction
    (D) The city's bus tour

39. What does the man say is included in the price?
    (A) An accommodation rate
    (B) A bus fare
    (C) All admission fees
    (D) The additional fee

40. According to the man, what should the woman bring tomorrow?
    (A) A leaflet
    (B) A receipt
    (C) A schedule
    (D) A guide map

41. What are the speakers talking about?
    (A) Shop opening
    (B) Parking area renewal
    (C) Street sign installation
    (D) Installatioin of new plumbing pipes

42. Why does the woman say she is worried?
    (A) The parking area will close during the construction.
    (B) Fewer customers will visit the store
    (C) The water supply will be cut off in the shopping mall.
    (D) An announcement will be distributed to the customers.

43. What does the man suggest?
    (A) To renew the rent lease
    (B) To notify the schedule to the shop owners
    (C) To download the map
    (D) To update information online

44. What is the conversation mainly about?

(A) Donating the fund
(B) Increasing the cost
(C) Thanking some contributors
(D) Buying the umbrellas

45. Why does the woman say, "I don't mind"?

(A) To ignore his apology.
(B) To show her interest
(C) To agree to his proposal.
(D) To remind him of his appointment.

46. Where does the man say he will contact?

(A) A shipping department
(B) A postal office
(C) A law firm
(D) A customer satisfaction center

47. What does the woman want to do?

(A) To buy a new laptop
(B) To hold a used charger
(C) To get a battery replacement
(D) To know manufacturer's phone number

48. Why is the woman surprised?

(A) Because of the expensive price
(B) Because there are no extra batteries
(C) Because of some other brands
(D) Because of the fame of the Xiaomi factory

49. What will the man probably do next?

(A) He will visit the Xiaomi storage room.
(B) He will replace his laptop with the new one.
(C) He will check the store stock.
(D) He will transmit 150 dollars to the manufacturer.

50. What problem does the woman report?

(A) The pipe has a leak.
(B) The room light doesn't turn on.
(C) The shower doesn't drain.
(D) The water is overflowing.

51. What does the man mean when he says, "In that case"?

(A) If you don't have enough time to wait for repairing
(B) If you meet your friends
(C) If we send a repairman to your room
(D) If we hear about your problem

52. What will the woman probably do next?

(A) Go to another room
(B) Check out of the hotel
(C) Meet the repairman
(D) Receive the refund

53. What problem does the man mention?

(A) Acquiring the outsourcing company
(B) Purchasing more trucks
(C) Putting an order in place
(D) A lack of larger trucks

54. According to Ms. Whitney, how does she know Mr. Buford Young?

(A) She was Mr. Buford Young's colleague before.
(B) She introduced Mr. Buford Young to Mr. Osawaldo.
(C) She drove Mr. Buford Young to a waiting area.
(D) She hasn't received Mr. Buford Young's e-mail.

55. By when will the speakers most likely receive a response from Mr. Buford Young?

(A) By 9:00 A.M.
(B) By 1:00 A.M.
(C) By 12:00 P.M.
(D) By 6:00 P.M.

56. Where will the men go tomorrow morning?

(A) To a theater
(B) To a musical instrument store
(C) To an art museum
(D) To the ticket box

57. Where will Ms. Kate Windsor meet Mr. Bruno Crawford and Mr. Dale Emory?

(A) At a historical site
(B) At a bus stop
(C) At the tourist information center
(D) At a hotel

58. What is Ms. Kate Windsor's job?

(A) A museum curator
(B) A ticket seller
(C) A bus driver
(D) A tour guide

---

59. What are the speakers discussing?

(A) A fundraising event
(B) A sales campaign
(C) A marketing strategy
(D) A refund policy

60. What do the men imply about the operation?

(A) It can receive more donations.
(B) It should have decreased business cost.
(C) It depended more on phone calls.
(D) It broke a record.

61. What kind of media will be most useful for donations?

(A) Online
(B) Telephone
(C) Direct mail
(D) Mobile phone

Price Table

| Seat Section, Ranked by Luxury Level | Price |
|---|---|
| Premium Class | $200 |
| First Class | $150 |
| Business class | $120 |
| Economy Class | $90 |

62. What does the woman ask the man to do?

(A) To schedule a bus
(B) To find a terminal
(C) To fix a regulation
(D) To open a bank account

63. What does the woman say is significant?

(A) Arriving at her house
(B) Booking a hotel
(C) Sending her documents
(D) Participating in a meeting

64. Look at the graphic. Where will the woman be seated on the bus?

(A) Premium Class
(B) First Class
(C) Business class
(D) Economy Class

GO ON TO THE NEXT PAGE

## Feeding Schedule

| Animal | Time |
|--------|------|
| Squirrel | 09:00 |
| Zebra | 09:30 |
| Goat | 10:00 |
| Rabbit | 10:30 |

## TABLE OF PRICE

| PRODUCT NUMBER | UNIT PRICE |
|----------------|------------|
| ME633 | $199.00 |
| JR956 | $55.00 |
| YO723 | $60.00 |
| IT512 | $65.00 |
| HI897 | $70.00 |
| SA249 | $75.00 |

65. What does the woman say about the guide map?

(A) It contains the route to the exit.
(B) It has no information on feeding times.
(C) It doesn't offer many interesting attractions.
(D) It can be found in the entrance.

66. Look at the graphic. Which animal feeding will the woman see?

(A) Squirrel
(B) Zebra
(C) Goat
(D) Rabbit

67. What does the man say about today's admission fee?

(A) 30 dollars
(B) 9 dollars
(C) Paid by only adults
(D) All tickets are free for today.

68. What did Mr. Judson Cranford send to Ms. Wilmer?

(A) A stock list
(B) A financial report
(C) A sales contract
(D) An e-mail

69. What problem does the woman mention?

(A) Her shipment has not arrived yet.
(B) Her order can't be fulfilled.
(C) Her meeting was canceled.
(D) Her appointment has not been made.

70. Look at the graphic. How much will the woman pay for her choice?

(A) $50.00
(B) $60.00
(C) $70.00
(D) $75.00

**Directions:** You will hear some talks given by a single speaker. You will be asked to answer three questions about what the speakers say in each talk. Select the best response to each question and mark the letter (A), (B), (C), or (D) on your answer sheet. The talks will not be printed in your test book and will be spoken only one time.

71. What field does the speaker most likely work in?

   (A) Sports entertainment
   (B) Fair site rent
   (C) Health care industry
   (D) Hospital construction

72. What will Dr. Woolley address in her speech?

   (A) How to use the medical technology
   (B) How to find a good place
   (C) How to consult the patients
   (D) How to entertain the spectators

73. Why are the listeners encouraged to stay after the presentation?

   (A) To contact hospital officials
   (B) To stay in Austin
   (C) To speak to Dr. Woolley
   (D) To go to the workshop

74. Why are the listeners invited to attend the meeting?

   (A) To listen to many complaints
   (B) To welcome the employees
   (C) To act by themselves
   (D) To learn how to solve a problem

75. What does the man mean when he says "I'll tell you what"?

   (A) He will end the conference.
   (B) He can tell them all the details about the new regulation.
   (C) He is going to give some suggestions.
   (D) He would like to know what is in the boxes.

76. What is Ms. Jessie Ward's job?

   (A) An architect
   (B) An expert in ecology
   (C) A hotel manager
   (D) A receptionist

77. Who most likely is the speaker?

   (A) A volunteer of this season
   (B) A manager of last season
   (C) An official of Jacksonville city
   (D) A director of the festival

78. According to the speaker, why are many visitors expected next Friday?

   (A) Because there will be an exciting concert
   (B) Because many volunteers will help the event go well
   (C) Because Jacksonville city will provide the best location
   (D) Because many tickets have already sold out

79. What does the speaker ask for help with?

   (A) Finishing the lines with people
   (B) Confirming at the ticket booth
   (C) Giving a call to Ms. Amy Smith
   (D) Using Mr. Kosby's mobile phone

80. What is the speaker trying to do?

   (A) To discuss customers' feedback
   (B) To guarantee the quality of the service
   (C) To suggest the excellent interior window
   (D) To negotiate a price

81. What service does Boykins offer?

   (A) Mailing
   (B) Feedback
   (C) Scheduling
   (D) Office cleaning

82. Why does the speaker say that he wants to hire Boykins agency?

   (A) Because it has a long history
   (B) Because it has a good reputation
   (C) Because it is a low price
   (D) Because it includes a total service

*GO ON TO THE NEXT PAGE*

83. What is the purpose of the announcement?

(A) To inform that Federico Corporated is the candidate for the Best Global Manufacturing Association Award
(B) To thank the Best Global Manufacturing Association
(C) To celebrate the award ceremony
(D) To nominate Federico Corporated

84. What does Federico Corporated produce?

(A) Doors for indoor use
(B) Electric power tools
(C) Rechargeable batteries
(D) Convenient energy exchanger

85. What does Federico Corporated plan to do next year?

(A) It will vote for the Best Global Manufacturing Association Award.
(B) It will provide users with the products of other brands.
(C) It will introduce a new line of a power tools.
(D) It will open its branch office in Panama.

86. Where most likely is the announcement taking place?

(A) An office
(B) A newspaper company
(C) A supermarket
(D) An advertising company

87. Which of the following information was wrong?

(A) Addington's location
(B) Shopping needs
(C) Booklet
(D) Sale price

88. What is available at the customer service desk?

(A) Seasonal fruits
(B) Some recipes
(C) Thank you cards
(D) The store's desserts

89. What problem does the speaker mention about George Investment?

(A) The time of the conference
(B) The number of attendants
(C) The location building project
(D) Its demand for a lower price

90. Why does the speaker say, "There's just one problem"?

(A) To inform the project completed
(B) To say the problem again
(C) To introduce a different issue
(D) To accept the demand of George Investment

91. What are the listeners asked to do?

(A) To confirm their future job
(B) To operate the equipment for the job
(C) To review the job details
(D) To complete the project form

92. What is the talk mainly about?

(A) The member of its municipal planning committee
(B) The discussion regarding the old school
(C) The construction on Rainier road
(D) The next agenda of a school committee

93. According to the speaker, what are residents concerned about?

(A) The school in a shopping center
(B) The decrease in an apartment complex
(C) The inconvenient commute of local people
(D) The increase in the price of rent

94. What does the speaker propose?

(A) To request that the local people change the school
(B) To invite both interested developers to the next meeting
(C) To ask some residents to rent in that area
(D) To conclude the exchange to permit

Morning Schedule

| Guide | Bus | Persons |
|-------|-------|---------|
| Baker | Bus 1 | 31 |
| Nichol | Bus 2 | 12 |
| Turner | Bus 3 | 9 |
| David | Bus 4 | 20 |

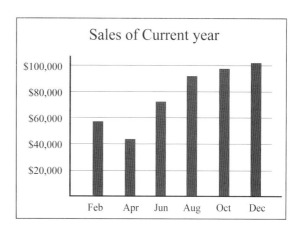

Sales of Current year

95. What will the listeners probably do this morning?
   (A) Attend a conference
   (B) Announce their needs
   (C) Wear yellow caps
   (D) Provide tours

96. According to the speaker, why did they change David's bus?
   (A) The number of people in the group has gotten smaller.
   (B) It has scored lower.
   (C) It has been out of order.
   (D) It has brought attention.

97. Look at the graphic. Which bus will David use?
   (A) Bus 1
   (B) Bus 2
   (C) Bus 3
   (D) Bus 4

98. Who will the woman probably be?
   (A) A marketing director
   (B) A general manager
   (C) An accountant
   (D) A lawyer

99. Why does the woman thank the sales department?
   (A) They created new ways to sell products.
   (B) They presented their outstanding jobs.
   (C) They looked at a graph of production.
   (D) They drove their vehicles to the station well.

100. Look at the graphic. What does the woman imply about sales next January?
   (A) They will be under $40,000.
   (B) They will reach $60,000.
   (C) They will increase $80,000.
   (D) They will exceed $100,000.

**This is the end of the Listening test. Turn to Part 5 in your text book.**

*GO ON TO THE NEXT PAGE*

## READING TEST

In the Reading test, you will read a variety of texts and answer several different types of reading comprehension questions. The entire Reading test will last 75 minutes. There are three parts, and directions are given for each part. You are encouraged to answer as many questions as possible within the time allowed.

You must mark your answers on the separate answer sheet. Do not write your answers in your test book.

## PART 5

**Directions:** A word or phrase is missing in each of the sentences below. Four answer choices are given below each sentence. Select the best answer to complete the sentence. Then mark the letter (A), (B), (C), or (D) on your answer sheet.

101. The LCD monitor delivered yesterday was ------- damaged, so we request that you send us another.

(A) accident
(B) accidents
(C) accidental
(D) accidentally

102. Mr. Corner Thompson was entertaining, funny, ------- and passionate, even if not a gentleman.

(A) engage
(B) engaged
(C) engaging
(D) engages

103. Modern design, which is much more sympathetic to the surroundings, lends ------- to the renovation of the countryside.

(A) it
(B) its
(C) itself
(D) them

104. If you have recently ------- an order with us, but you have not yet received it, you must first check with us to see whether or not it has been sent.

(A) took
(B) had
(C) filed
(D) placed

105. Ms. Lisa Brook has organized the fundraising event and actively ------- large corporate donations to support the family entertainment center.

(A) offered
(B) received
(C) allowed
(D) solicited

106. The huge amount of cash has led to the ------- of national investment funds.

(A) emergency
(B) origin
(C) emergence
(D) cause

107. The salary of the permanent positions will rise but ------- of the temporary positions will be reduced.

(A) that
(B) this
(C) it
(D) those

108. Your blunt words have broken their ------- in you, but warning them in advance will strengthen their trust.

(A) confide
(B) confidence
(C) confident
(D) confidently

14

**109.** My colleagues and I would like to sincerely express ------- appreciation for your frequent purchases.

(A) my
(B) our
(C) your
(D) their

**110.** The Current Trend Research is considering researching its recent findings in further ------- and is planning to write a follow up report shortly

(A) deep
(B) deeply
(C) deepen
(D) depth

**111.** Mr. Eric Schmidt had brought special ------- into Google's history and corporate's spirit before he recently retired.

(A) collaboration
(B) authorization
(C) right
(D) insight

**112.** If you want to print out the required documents for the entire project, you should first enroll ------- this web-site.

(A) for
(B) at
(C) in
(D) on

**113.** After reading The Customer Comes magazine, I was really amazed and I think you ------- a minute to review The Customer Comes magazine.

(A) take
(B) should take
(C) will take
(D) would be taking

**114.** Although it has sought to make the banking system stable, the bonus issue has been a huge ------- for the government.

(A) concentration
(B) distraction
(C) conglomeration
(D) separation

**115.** Since we ------- Pine Apply Ltd. guarantee the quality of our items, all of our merchandise is completely reliable.

(A) on
(B) in
(C) at
(D) to

**116.** All small business owners should know what their rivals are doing before they establish -------.

(A) herself
(B) himself
(C) itself
(D) themselves

**117.** The manager will ------- extra paperwork to a senior reporter due to the promotion of a new line.

(A) change
(B) earn
(C) assign
(D) acquire

**118.** The ------- applicants should have a master's degree in pharmacy and at least two letters of recommendation.

(A) qualify
(B) qualifies
(C) qualifying
(D) qualified

**119.** An e-mail will be automatically forwarded to you ------- the item you ordered becomes available.

(A) as soon as
(B) when
(C) while
(D) after

**120.** Not long after I purchased a G3 phone in May 2024, the screen died, so I contacted LS mobile about receiving a -------.

(A) replace
(B) replacing
(C) replaced
(D) replacement

*GO ON TO THE NEXT PAGE*

121. Thunder Supply Co., known as a leading manufacturing company, may hire the ------- candidates, most of whom majored marketing or related fields.
(A) interview
(B) interviews
(C) interviewed
(D) interviewing

122. The product will be delivered only ------- bilateral confirmation and agreement to the completion of comprehensive testing.
(A) as soon as
(B) immediately
(C) directly
(D) upon

123. ------- was a remarkable increase in the number of vehicles outside the museum because the newly constructed department store is located nearby.
(A) There
(B) It
(C) They
(D) Those

124. Sales of the new products are expected to increase as summer ------- approaches.
(A) vacation
(B) season
(C) time
(D) period

125. Computer technology is utilized throughout the school and students are instructed in ------- ways to enhance their writing.
(A) effect
(B) effective
(C) effectiveness
(D) effectively

126. The ------- entry will be published in the property section of the daily newspaper Telegraph and the video will appear on Telegraph TV.
(A) win
(B) won
(C) winning
(D) wins

127. Heavy pollution from fatal chemicals resulted in the disruption of the mating behavior of snakes, leading to an ------- decline in their population.
(A) enough
(B) amusing
(C) extreme
(D) exciting

128. We look forward to finding out more about the company ------- the next shareholder's meeting.
(A) onto
(B) into
(C) during
(D) upon

129. Even frequent flyers may have to pay ------- charges for flying during peak seasons.
(A) overlapped
(B) regular
(C) single
(D) double

130. The shipment you ordered last weekend will be received ------- today or tomorrow.
(A) both
(B) not
(C) either
(D) neither

## PART 6

**Directions:** Read the texts that follow. A word, phrase, or sentence is missing in parts of each text. Four answer choices for each question are given below the text. Select the best answer to complete the text. Then mark the letter (A), (B), (C), or (D) on your answer sheet.

**Questions 131-134** refer to the following information.

McMaster University is a first-class institution ------- students from over many provinces in
**131.**
Canada boast their scholastic achievements. McMaster University ------- more heavily on
**132.**
private contributions than on public money.

The proposed center was first suggested by students and faculty, who thought that the

center should have a swimming pool and an exercise facility.

We hope to build the center in order to attract international students. To remain -------, it is
**133.**
important that we avoid raising tuition to pay for the construction of the facility. -------.
**134.**

Donors' names will be inscribed on a marble tablet which will be set into the walls of

the front entranceway of the center, and which will be uncovered at a public dedication

ceremony.

131. (A) which
(B) who
(C) whom
(D) whose

132. (A) depends
(B) concentrates
(C) belongs
(D) results

133. (A) compete
(B) competitive
(C) competitively
(D) competition

134. (A) We should raise tuition to attract
much more students
(B) The total funding amount needed is
$8.6 million
(C) We hope to build the center where
donors' names will be inscribed
(D) We expressed our opinion that
McMaster University should give
students a scholarship

GO ON TO THE NEXT PAGE

**How to Remove Clutter From a Hard Drive**

It can be hard to find what you're looking for if your hard disk is full of unneeded files.

Just like with your paper filing cabinet. Do ------- a favor sometime and weed out
**135.**

unnecessary stuff.

Applications and Documents

Steps:

» First) Open your document and applications folders.

» Second) Drag the icons for unneeded documents to the Recycle Bin

» Third) Back up documents you want to keep

» Fourth) Move ------- documents to the Recycle Bin after you've backed them up.
**136.**

» Fifth) Empty your Recycle Bin after completing the above steps.

» Sixth) Remove ------- application programs by using an installer program. In Windows,
**137.**

use the Add/Remove in control panel. On the Mac, many installer programs include a

Remove option.

Tips:

Application programs typically put files in your Windows or System folders in addition to

what you see in the application folder itself; that's why uninstaller programs are helpful.

-------. Sound, graphics and especially video files take up much more.
**138.**

135. (A) myself
(B) ourselves
(C) yourself
(D) themselves

136. (A) this
(B) that
(C) these
(D) those

137. (A) purchased
(B) copied
(C) unauthorized
(D) unwanted

138. (A) Text files don't take up much space
on a disk
(B) Text files must not occupy much
amount on a memory stick
(C) Text files should be located in a hard
disk
(D) Text files should be examined for safe
use

The international economy is not stable, and for many people job-hunting has become a lifestyle. With mergers, takeovers, bankruptcies, and new government legislations, you could become unemployed overnight, even if you own the company.

Make it a ------- to let your network of recruiters, personal friends, and business
         **139.**
acquaintances know where you are and what you're doing, at all times, especially when you change jobs or addresses. Announce changes even if it's an inter-company move.

------- they land a job, ex-job-hunters tend to forget those who've helped them. They
   **140.**
get busy packing, moving, tying up loose ends, and taking on the duties of the new assignment, but that's a mistake. Remember, your first duty is to maintain your relationships. This doesn't mean that your new assignment isn't important. It means that your friendships and your personal future are also equally important.

The ------- way to handle the thank-you task is to give the letters and mailing list to a
    **141.**
secretarial service. Let them type and address the letters; and you sign them. -------.
                                                                          **142.**

Believe me, it's time well spent.

---

139. (A) priority
     (B) preference
     (C) rule
     (D) pleasure

140. (A) If
     (B) Unless
     (C) Once
     (D) When

141. (A) quick
     (B) quicker
     (C) quickly
     (D) quickest

142. (A) This asks you to work hard with your time and energy
     (B) This requires very little time and energy, probably less than two hours
     (C) This encourages you to sign them a letter with your address
     (D) This prevents you from giving your letter and mailing list to a secretarial service

GO ON TO THE NEXT PAGE

Questions 143-146 refer to the following advertisement.

---

# JOB OPPORTUNITY

The Assistance for the Youth is a non-profit organization that provides the unemployed with meaningful work in the area of business. The Assistance for the Youth is now accepting applications for the following position :

## FINANCE & ADMINISTRATION MANAGER

-------. A qualified financial specialist should apply for the position of accounting director.
**143.**
An applicant should be able to handle a current accounting system to maintain accurate records, to prepare regular financial annual reports, ------- those required for annual
**144.**
auditing, and to process payroll for all employees. This individual will also oversee various administrative duties ------- the Assistance for the Youth's operations.
**145.**

## Qualifications:

» 4-year diploma or more than a 6-year degree in Business Administration with focus in finance or equivalent ------- experience
**146.**

» experience and knowledge of The Assistance for the Youth's programs will be considered an asset

This position is a two-year renewable contractual position.

Salary will be based on qualifications and experience.

---

**143.** (A) We search for a potential candidate who would like to work independently
(B) We ask the monetary specialist to accept the open position
(C) We need an energetic team player for the financial functions
(D) We prepare regular financial reports and annual auditing statements

**144.** (A) considering
(B) including
(C) excluding
(D) regarding

**145.** (A) according to
(B) owing to
(C) depending on
(D) pertaining to

**146.** (A) work
(B) works
(C) working
(D) worked

**Directions:** In this part you will read a selection of texts, such as magazine and newspaper articles, e-mails, and instant messages. Each text or set of texts is followed by several questions. Select the best answer for each question and mark the letter (A), (B), (C), or (D) on your answer sheet.

**Questions 147-148** refer to the following advertisement.

### ONNet introduces its NEW DSLite!

DSLite NITRO    $100.00 per month (includes internet costs)

**BENEFITS:**

1. DSLite is always on - Just click on the internet browser icon on your computer, and start surfing the internet!
2. Up to 10 times faster than previous dial up service!
3. It is possible to talk on the phone and surf the Internet simultaneously - you don't need to use a second phone line!
4. No busy signals!
5. No more failed and dropped connections!
6. Faster uploads and downloads!
7. Multiple computers on a single DSLite line!

When you join this service, we'll throw in a free keyboard.

Contact Information
Tel: 532-765-5842  E-mail: dslite@onnet.com

147. What is being advertised?
(A) A newly published computer manual
(B) A new Internet connection service
(C) A free Internet phone service
(D) A state-of-the-art computer

148. What is NOT a stated advantage of this service?
(A) The speed is far faster than that of existent services.
(B) The service is available at all times.
(C) Users can talk on the phone while web surfing.
(D) One computer is available on a single line.

GO ON TO THE NEXT PAGE

Questions 149-150 refer to the following text message chain.

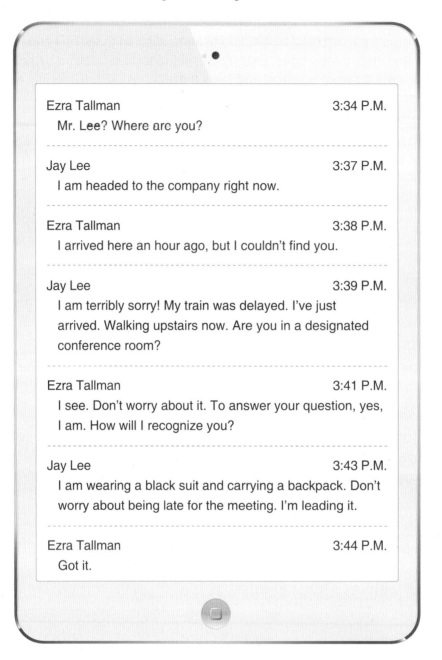

Ezra Tallman                                          3:34 P.M.
  Mr. Lee? Where are you?

- - - - - - - - - - - - - - - - - - - - - - - - - - - - - - - - - - - - -

Jay Lee                                              3:37 P.M.
  I am headed to the company right now.

- - - - - - - - - - - - - - - - - - - - - - - - - - - - - - - - - - - - -

Ezra Tallman                                          3:38 P.M.
  I arrived here an hour ago, but I couldn't find you.

- - - - - - - - - - - - - - - - - - - - - - - - - - - - - - - - - - - - -

Jay Lee                                              3:39 P.M.
  I am terribly sorry! My train was delayed. I've just
  arrived. Walking upstairs now. Are you in a designated
  conference room?

- - - - - - - - - - - - - - - - - - - - - - - - - - - - - - - - - - - - -

Ezra Tallman                                          3:41 P.M.
  I see. Don't worry about it. To answer your question, yes,
  I am. How will I recognize you?

- - - - - - - - - - - - - - - - - - - - - - - - - - - - - - - - - - - - -

Jay Lee                                              3:43 P.M.
  I am wearing a black suit and carrying a backpack. Don't
  worry about being late for the meeting. I'm leading it.

- - - - - - - - - - - - - - - - - - - - - - - - - - - - - - - - - - - - -

Ezra Tallman                                          3:44 P.M.
  Got it.

149. What is true about Ms. Ezra Tallman and
Mr. Jay Lee?

(A) They used different modes of
transportation.
(B) They are waiting for the same client.
(C) They have never met before.
(D) They have once worked in the same
company.

150. At 3:44 P.M., why does Ms. Ezra Tallman
say "Got it"?

(A) To give the information to Mr. Jay Lee
(B) To emphasize the importance of the
conference
(C) To apologize for being late for the
meeting
(D) To express the understanding of Mr.
Jay Lee's comment

**Questions 151-152** refer to the following information.

---

## *Virus Alert*

AntiVirusProtect protects you against AVP WEBSITE.

Viruses such as the "Worm" use the Visual Basic Scripting language. This is a strong language with unchecked abilities in Outlook and Outlook Express. AlphaBase AntiVirusProtect guarantees that a user knows before a AVPScript is executed. After installing AntiVirusProtect Program, the user is provided the choice to execute the script or to stop before any potential damage occurs. We offer you AntiVirusProtect as an additional antivirus software. It doesn't depend on a fingerprint of an existing virus, it prompts you for permission before any Visual Basic Script is executed.

**Note:** The Windows Scripting Host (WSH) consists of Visual Basic Scripts. Users who don't use WSH don't need to use this software. The standard installations of Internet Explorer version 6.0, Windows Vista, and Windows XP install WSH. In Windows NT and Windows 2000, WSH is provided as an option. AntiVirusProtect enables the user to control the execution of these scripts on their computer. AntiVirusProtect is Free software for everyone.

---

**151.** What is offered to users after setting up AntiVirusProtect?

(A) Installation of the Visual Basic Scripting language

(B) A choice of either executing the script or ceasing

(C) Use of the Visual Basic Scripting language

(D) No more worries about viruses any more

**152.** What is NOT true about this information?

(A) There are viruses which don't use the Visual Basic Scripting language.

(B) AntiVirusProtect has its own way to search for an existing virus without counting on a fingerprint.

(C) AntiVirusProtect lets users choose whether or not to activate any Visual Basic Script.

(D) WSH should be installed in Windows NT and Windows 2000.

*GO ON TO THE NEXT PAGE*

From : Raymond Murphy
To : Melvin Cransey
Subject : Finalized Leasing Agreement

Dear Ms. Cransey :

I celebrate the recent grand opening of your shop!
We are pleased that you selected our company to lease facilities and equipment
from and we hope that your venture will go well.
As requested, a signed copy of the lease agreement has been enclosed in this
mail. The copy will extend your lease an additional five months beyond the original
lease. Please sign and date the document and send it back to me. If you want to
know further details or have any questions or concerns about the enclosed lease
agreement, please don't hesitate to call. You can reach me at (533) 494-9439 or stop
by our office.
If there are any additional services that we can offer now or in the future, please feel
free to call on us. We hope that our company will work with you again in the future.
All of us at Murphy Cat Furniture really enjoyed working with you and your team.
Best of luck on your new venture!
Sincerely,

Raymond Murphy
Vice President, Murphy Cat Furniture

153. What is attached in this e-mail?
  (A) A joint venture
  (B) Fittings rental agreement
  (C) A company acquisition
  (D) Land lease contract

154. Why did Mr. Raymond Murphy write this e-mail?
  (A) To thank Cransey for the satisfactory condition of the facilities
  (B) To protest a violation of the lease agreement
  (C) To confirm a phone number on the contract
  (D) To send the revised lease contract

# ARE YOU ONE OF THOSE CHRONIC SPENDERS?

You've heard about those who rack up $15,000 in credit card debt just because they "had to have" that new pair of boots for fall or the newest smart phone. Most people would think, "What a fool. I'd never be so silly." --- [1] ---. Well, maybe not. Eventually, you might also have those new things, and you might manage to maintain your bank account in the black and your debt in check. However, keeping your bank account in the black doesn't mean you're not a chronic spender. Most chronic spending is often unconscious spending, so you may not even know you are a chronic spender. --- [2] ---.

There are some relatively simple methods you can use to reduce your chronic spending, if not stop it entirely. "Most people who are spending unconsciously tend to make spending mistakes in a specific, recurring area," Mr. Kim said. To know where you are, he recommends going through your home and taking an inventory of what you own. For example, when you look through your shoes cabinet and you find 30 pairs of shoes, only four of which you usually wear, you should make a mental note to stop buying shoes for the time being. --- [3] ---.

Another method is to put yourself on a 1-month spending moratorium, Ms. Lee said. Use only cash to buy basic necessities like food and write down every penny you spend. Most people who try this exercise don't just stick to the basics, she said, so it's helpful to see where you make chronic spending. --- [4] ---.

Ms. Lee recommends to try practicing living with a budget smaller than your income. She suggests allocating your earnings in the following way: 70 percent for living purchases and expenses ;  10 percent for charity and 20 percent for savings.

The savings and charity portions of your income "stop those insatiable desires," she said, since your eyes can be open to the world's needs and to your long-term financial security.

155. What advice is given to find out where one spends unnecessary money?

(A) Meet shop owners
(B) Go through his/her house
(C) Read books on wise spending
(D) Compare his/her expenditure with others

156. What does Ms. Lee recommend as a way of restricting chronic spending?

(A) Not spending even a penny
(B) Practice living with a lower income
(C) Save up one's whole salary
(D) Budget living expenses carefully

157. In which of the positions marked [1], [2], [3] and [4] does the following sentence best belong?

"Therefore, you must check whether or not you are chronic spender."

(A) [1]
(B) [2]
(C) [3]
(D) [4]

GO ON TO THE NEXT PAGE

## Private Surfing Lessons Beginning from $100 per person
Duration : 2 hr. 20 min., Location : San Francisco, California

INTRODUCTION

Los Angeles is famous for a beautiful coastline, white beaches and a big surfing community, so what better place to ride some waves? For people who aren't experienced surfers, you can have expert instructors teach you the fundamental steps of surfing, so you'll be standing on the board in no time!

Safety and fun are very important things in all lessons, but they also take the next stage and teach their students to see the ocean with a surfer's eye in order for them to surf safely with confidence and enjoy the waves.

DEPARTURE AND RETURN SCHEDULE

- Departure Dates : Daily – June 11, 2024 to June 30, 2024
- Indoor Lesson Place : Lessons are held at Queen Avenue, Los Angeles Beach
- Departure Time : Departure time is reliant on ocean and tide conditions, but is normally around 10:00 A.M. Accurate time to be confirmed 48 hours prior to lesson
- Hotel Pickup : We don't provide this service.

ADDITIONAL INCLUSIONS :
- Surfboard Rental
- Wetsuit Rental
- Private Surfing Lesson
- Lunch costs

EXCLUSIONS :
- Parking Fees
- Gratuities (Optional)

**158.** Who would be most interested in this advertisement?

(A) Residents in San Francisco
(B) A member of the professional surfing community in San Francisco
(C) Instructors teaching surf-riding to beginners
(D) People who have never surfed in the sea

**159.** When might be possible for students to take the lesson?

(A) At 11:30 A.M. on July 20, 2024
(B) At 5:00 A.M. on June 22, 2024
(C) At 11:00 A.M. on July 1. 2024
(D) At 11:00 A.M. on June 15, 2024

**160.** Which of the following is true about this private surfing lesson?

(A) Students can surf by themselves without the instructor's help in 30 minutes.
(B) UDS is the most well-known surfing school in California.
(C) Students don't need to prepare wetsuit.
(D) This lesson must be booked at least 72 hours in advance.

**Questions 161-163** refer to the following introduction.

## The Way to Pay by Money Order or Check

We appreciate you for your interest in purchasing SiGe HBT items through mail with a business, personal check, or by money order.

We are very familiar with these type of payments and have provided our clients with this service for over 10 years.

**Make sure you include :**

1. A money order or check made payable to: SiGe HBT
2. Include the shipping charges stated (if applicable)
3. Please let us know if your order is for a downloadable type, or if you need the item on a CD-ROM (note: a few items are not downloadable in which case we will deliver the CD-ROM instead - see each item in detail on the website to find out if the downloadable version is available)
4. If you order a CD, please let us know the exact address to deliver the CD to.
5. Please give us an e-mail address so that we can let you know that your payment was received and the item has been shipped.

**Shipping Prices :**

We offer all clients in Canada priority mail shipping service for free no matter how many items are ordered. The shipping will take 3 to 5 business days. International clients outside of the Canada who are ordering a CD, must include $30.00 for the international shipping cost.

You don't need to pay for shipping if you ordered a downloadable item.

When the above information is complete, send payment to :

SiGe HBT
240 Neal Dr
Scarborough, Ontario 39442

All orders are processed promptly after the money or check order is received. If you have a question, please contact our billing team. Then our billing team will help you immediately.

---

**161.** What form of billing does the company NOT receive?

(A) Money order
(B) Individual check
(C) Cash
(D) Company check

**162.** What should be included when ordering the product?

(A) A telephone number
(B) The name of the product
(C) Cash payable to SiGe HBT
(D) A shipping fee

**163.** When will the customers receive the product?

(A) After they download the CD
(B) After sending the payment
(C) After 3-5 business days
(D) After sending $30

*GO ON TO THE NEXT PAGE*

Questions 164-167 refer to the following text message chain.

| Text Message | _ □ × |

| **Lindsay Wagner**<br>11:45 A.M. | When will you arrive? I met our customer, Ms. Nunez, in the reception desk a few minutes ago. |
| **Rob Murphy**<br>11:47 A.M. | My bus is stuck in traffic. I haven't moved for 20 minutes. |
| **Lindsay Wagner**<br>11:48 A.M. | No. Our arrangement with Ms. Nunez is scheduled start at 12:00. What should I do? Make her wait? |
| **Rob Murphy**<br>11:50 A.M. | No. She said she only has until 1:00 P.M. today, so please start without me. |
| **Lindsay Wagner**<br>11:52 A.M. | But I don't know how to introduce our new services to her. |
| **Rob Murphy**<br>11:53 A.M. | Sure, you do. You're the one who put the presentation together. You start, and I'll join in when I get there. It'll be fine. |
| **Lindsay Wagner**<br>11:54 A.M. | I'll do my best. |
| **Rob Murphy**<br>11:56 A.M. | The bus just started moving again. Hopefully, I'll get there around 12:30. I'll come straight to the conference room. |
| **Lindsay Wagner**<br>11:58 A.M. | Please do. I'm on my way to greet Ms. Nunez now. |

| Send |

164. Why is Rob Murphy' bus stopped?

(A) Because of construction
(B) Because of a car accident
(C) Because of a traffic jam
(D) Because of a traffic checkpoint

165. At 11:53 A.M., what does Rob Murphy mean when he writes, "Sure, you do"?

(A) He wants Lindsay Wagner to introduce Ms. Nunez to him.
(B) He believes Ms. Nunez will place an order.
(C) He guesses the conference will begin on time.
(D) He thinks Lindsay Wagner can give the presentation herself.

166. What is indicated about Ms. Nunez?

(A) Her time is confined.
(B) She is a coworker of Mr. Rob Murphy.
(C) She is satisfied with her company's new services.
(D) Her bus is stuck in traffic.

167. What will Ms. Lindsay Wagner do next?

(A) Greet Rob Murphy
(B) Welcome her client
(C) Get off the bus
(D) Reschedule her arrangement

GO ON TO THE NEXT PAGE

ABC International Chinese Language Schools

--- [1] ---. Welcome to ABC International Chinese Language Schools. ABC has a good reputation for high academic standards world-wide and they offer many activity programs. ABC institute is a Chinese owned organization. We never close except on public holidays. Our language schools are located in downtown Beijing and Shanghai. Students can transfer schools between the two cities. --- [2] ---.

There is a maximum of nearly 200 students in each school: large enough to have 10 grade levels of Chinese; small enough for every student to befriend each other. There are Junior Language Schools in March, June, September, and December for students 10 to 18 years of age and Senior Schools for students 19 years of age and over. --- [3] ---.

At ABC Schools there is a kitchen where students are able to make simple meals (free coffee / tea is always available); a library and quiet area for studying Chinese; a recreational space with billiard tables and a piano; a multimedia center; and free access to internet. Also, there is a seminar room in the facility. ABC institute is government registered as a Private Training Program Establishment. We are a signatory to the Ministry of Education Code of Practice for the support of international students, recruitment, welfare for international students. --- [4] ---.

168. Who would be most interested in this brochure?

(A) People who want to enjoy tea at no cost
(B) 18 year olds who wish to learn cooking as a profession
(C) Overseas students searching for a Chinese school
(D) Australian students who want to learn foreign languages

169. What is not the reason why ABC is renowned worldwide?

(A) High academic standards
(B) A conveniently placed location
(C) Various activities
(D) A lovely relaxing atmosphere

170. Which of the following is true of ABC according to this brochure?

(A) There are 8 branch schools of ABC all around Australia.
(B) There are special courses for 10 to 18 year olds 4 months a year.
(C) Programs of ABC are only for people over 18 years old.
(D) Students can use computers as much as they want at reasonable rates.

171. In which of the positions marked [1], [2], [3] and [4] does the following sentence best belong?

"There is a Silvers Chinese Program for students 60 years and over."

(A) [1]
(B) [2]
(C) [3]
(D) [4]

GO ON TO THE NEXT PAGE

**Questions 172-175** refer to the following memo.

To: The Staff
From: [Managing editor] Sandra Farcon
Date: Mar. 30, 2024
Re: New measures

In Monday's paper, we published two articles that all of us wanted to publish a while ago, but couldn't until now. The articles are both stories regarding our errors in the "Something Under Fire" series. The stories go into detail about the causes of our mistakes, and how we can improve from them. In summary, there's no more time to lose. It's time to start moving forward. The problems specified in the stories should never happen again. We, as journalists, will do our best with what we learn from this experience. And we must find out how to make our newspaper even better. Through this memorandum, I will go over how we can improve further.

Here are the measures we will take:
We will focus additional attention on background checks, including renewed training methods on conducting effective surveys, and more active discussions during editing and reporting on when to start them, who conducts them, and how far to take them. Before a project is endorsed, senior editors will weigh and debate actively whether the project should be treated by reporters with specific subject-matter knowledge or by more than one reporter.

We should charge the primary editor of a project with the duty of ensuring timely and complete flow of information to senior editors on key developments, turning points or issues, including disagreements between the reporter and the primary editor. We will insist on the primary editor participating in all higher-level discussions including legal ones, as the lead project representative.

We will have to make sure for the reader, information sources and internal reactions to main projects or especially sensitive stories goes not only to the editors and reporters most closely involved in the story but also to the public editor. All things related to the project will be acted upon with due and proper speed.

Please keep in mind the facts above. Anika Merlin, Chales Lee, and I will work together to announce the next specific measures to take regarding each of these points in the following week. If you have any ideas or specific interests, please let us know. Call us at: 1-539-684-3023. Or you can visit our editor's office located on the 5th floor of the Casey Building.

**172.** What is the purpose of this memo?

(A) To blame especially idle editors who committed errors

(B) To advise of modifications designed to improve the newspaper

(C) To allocate new supervisors to each division

(D) To diffuse negative effects of errors they made

**173.** Which of the following should the senior editors do from now on?

(A) Settle the problems between reporters and readers.

(B) Manage all processes until the newspaper is published.

(C) Make a decision on who will undertake a project.

(D) Supervise reporters and photographers from each division.

**174.** What is NOT true about this memo?

(A) The story and the column on their mistakes were published in Monday's paper.

(B) The head of the company resented and directed special steps to improve the newspaper.

(C) 3 people will cooperate to conduct specific steps in the coming week.

(D) Someone who has ideas on the topic can drop by the office in person.

**175.** The words "key" line 2, paragraph 3, is closest in meaning to

(A) innovative

(B) huge

(C) productive

(D) important

GO ON TO THE NEXT PAGE

**Questions 176-180** refer to the following advertisement and e-mail.

Searching for a new venue to hold a gathering for your company? Looking for a great place that's fun for adults? Try Secret Garden, a place for office parties, team building, and small conferences.

Secret Garden offers small conference rooms that hold up to 50 people. We also have a banquet room that is great for parties, events, and large meetings. Rooms are complete with the newest projector, a high quality speaker system, and special lighting.

After your business meeting, enjoy a day of mini-golf with fresh refreshments. We offer a driving range upstairs and 18 holes of fun downstairs. Special company packages and rates for groups of 10 or more are available. Call 348-5763 for more information or e-mail info@secretgarden.com.

| From | Audrey Murphy <audrey@gmail.com> |
| --- | --- |
| To | info@secretgarden.com |
| Subject | Reservation |

To whom it may concern,

How are you? I am Audrey Murphy. I would like to make a reservation for your banquet room on Saturday, November 15 at 6 P.M. if it is available. The reservation should be under my name and is for Highways Inc.

There will be 300 people attending. I would also like some information on catering. I understand there is a restaurant at Secret Garden, but can we bring our own caterer? Also, what food is offered through your catering service?

Please get back to me as soon as possible. Although November is still two months away, we need to plan this party.

Thank you in advance,
Audrey Murphy
HR Manager

Human Resources Dept.
046-348-2064
Highways, Inc.
www.highways.com

176. What is NOT included in all rooms?

    (A) Speaker system
    (B) A projector
    (C) Special lighting
    (D) Free refreshments

177. What is upstairs at Secret Garden?

    (A) Cafe
    (B) Banquet hall
    (C) Driving range
    (D) Conference rooms

178. What room is Ms. Murphy reserving?

    (A) Ballroom
    (B) Banquet room
    (C) Small conference room
    (D) Large conference room

179. What is Ms. Murphy inquiring about?

    (A) Catering
    (B) Room sizes
    (C) Refreshments
    (D) Golf courses

180. What is Ms. Murphy's position at Highways Inc.?

    (A) Chief Secretary
    (B) Event Coordinator
    (C) Personal Assistant
    (D) Human Resources Manager

GO ON TO THE NEXT PAGE

| To | Food & Meal World |
| --- | --- |
| From | Linda Turner |
| Subject | recipe |

Dear Patricia Spencer,

I was eager to send you a thank you-note for everything you did for the party. The food was something that had to be just right, and everything your company did was perfect. The selection, appearance and timing were fantastic! My daughter (the bride) has been raving about the spinach that you served. Do you think you could tell me the recipe so I can give it to her? Perhaps as a wedding present?

Sincere thanks,
Linda Turner

| To | Linda Turner |
| --- | --- |
| From | Bianca Hamilton |
| Subject | Re: recipe |

Mrs. Linda Turner,

I am writing back to your e-mail on behalf of Patricia Spencer, who has taken a week-long vacation. It was our pleasure to be at such a wonderful reception. The recipe for the spinach, which is a popular side dish served with many different curry dishes, is as follows:

Spicy Spinach

Trim and thoroughly wash 1kg/2lbs fresh spinach. Cook a chopped onion, a crushed garlic clove, a teaspoon of turmeric and two tablespoons of cumin seeds in a little butter or oil. Add the spinach and cover the pan tightly, cooking for 10 minutes. The key is to uncover the pan for the final five minutes and shake often. When the liquid has evaporated, you're done! Enjoy your food!
Congratulations once again to your daughter on her marriage.

From all of us here on Food & Meal World Catering Service,
Bianca Hamilton

181. What is the main purpose of Linda Turner's e-mail?

(A) To complain about the catering
(B) To compliment the food service
(C) To inquire about a party
(D) To invite someone to a wedding

182. Who got married?

(A) Linda Turner
(B) Linda Turner's son
(C) Linda Turner's daughter
(D) Patricia Spencer's daughter

183. What did the bride like the most about the meal?

(A) The appearance
(B) The spinach
(C) The timing
(D) The curry dishes

184. Why did Bianca Hamilton reply to Linda Turner's e-mail?

(A) Because Patricia Spencer was out of the office.
(B) Because she is a friend of Linda Turner's.
(C) Because she is the head chef.
(D) Because she knew the recipe.

185. What is the most important part of the cooking process?

(A) Uncovering the pan
(B) Crushing the garlic
(C) Using 1kg/2lbs of spinach
(D) Adding the cumin seeds

GO ON TO THE NEXT PAGE

**Questions 186-190** refer to the following advertisement, form and e-mail.

### The Fresh start at Honolulu Beachside begins with Oahu Lands

The awesome performance by talented entertainer Bruno Khans

Opening Weekend performance Dates and Times :

#1. Friday, July 15, 7:30 P.M.

#2. Saturday, July 16, 2:30 P.M.

#3. Saturday, July 16, 7:30 P.M.

#4. Sunday, July 17, 1:00 P.M.

A preview performance (#0) will be held Wednesday, July 13 at 7:00 P.M.

* Seating is limited solely to Honolulu Beachside members and reviewers from local media.

* Either a membership card or press identification is required

Ticket Prices :

| | |
|---|---|
| Adults | $50 |
| Children (age 12 and under) | $40 |
| Groups (5 persons or more) | $45 |
| Secondary School | $42 |

* A 30% discount is applicable to Honolulu Beachside members.

Visit www.HonoluluBeachside.org for an online order form, or for more information.

### *Honolulu Beachside*

Oahu Lands Order form

| | |
|---|---|
| Name | Jackson Anderson |
| Membership account number | NQ8653126 |
| Performance number | #0 |
| Price | $150 |
| Number of ticket(s) | 5 |
| Address | 903 Keeaumoku St. Honolulu Hawaii 96815 |
| E-mail | jacksonan@ocr.us.com |

| From | customerservice@HonoluluBeachside.org |
| --- | --- |
| To | Jackson Anderson <jacksonan@ocr.us.com> |
| Date | May 29 |
| Subject | Tickets |

Dear Mr. Jackson Anderson,

I got your order by online on May 28 indicating that you prefer to buy tickets for the world premiere of Oahu Lands. However, tickets for the event are not available. All of t them sold out quickly.

If you would like to purchase tickets for a different day, please call me at 808-777-2123 as soon as possible, since the number of tickets is limited. However, you may not be able to get a discount on certain days.

Also, it seems like your membership has expired, so if you wish to renew your membership, please visit our website for membership renewal.

Best regards,

Silvia Machado

Director of Honolulu Beachside

* If you think you can make a contribution, no matter how small or great, you are always welcome.

---

**186.** What can be inferred about Mr. Bruno Khans?

(A) He has composed many songs.
(B) He will take part in the Wednesday performance.
(C) He has worked with Ms. Silvia Machado before.
(D) His song has been praised.

**187.** According to the advertisement, how much is a ticket for a 10-year-old?

(A) $50
(B) $45
(C) $42
(D) $40

**188.** When did Mr. Jackson Anderson want to see the event?

(A) July 13
(B) July 15
(C) July 16
(D) July 17

**189.** What is NOT implied about Honolulu Beachside?

(A) It offers reduced ticket prices to members.
(B) It accepts donation from people in the community.
(C) It provides identification badges to visitors.
(D) It hosts special performances for the press.

**190.** What is mentioned about Mr. Jackson Anderson?

(A) He will see a play on Wednesday.
(B) He has to report to Honolulu Beachside for a refund.
(C) He might be unable to receive a discount.
(D) His mobile phone is out of order.

*GO ON TO THE NEXT PAGE* ➡

**Questions 191-195** refer to the following advertisement, text message and e-mail.

 **For SALE**

TAYLOR log cabin in rural areas. The house has three floors, brick walls, and four bedrooms in a quiet neighborhood. Newly painted, inside and out. Established garden. Friendly neighborhood with shops nearby. 30 minutes by car from the train station. Primary school within easy walking distance. Call Mr. Mark Ashley at 475-755-7467, or e-mail him at markashley@forsale.org.

To : Mr. Mark Ashley

Hello, Mr. Mark Ashley.
We got a phone call from Ms. Dannie Moore who read the advertisement about the property. She said it sounds great, but she had a few questions. First, she wants to know if there is a high school and a middle school nearby, as her son finishes elementary school next year. Second, she asked whether there is enough space to park three cars. Third, she wants to know about the heating system for the winter. She left her mobile phone number, and would like you to call back after 6 P.M. tonight.

From : Ms. Lisa Brook

| To | Ms. Dannie Moore |
|---|---|
| From | Amy Forest |
| Subject | Re : cabin for sale |

Dear Ms. Dannie Moore,

I am so happy to hear the news about the neighborhood. It'll be a great change!

It's got three floors, right? Could you check and make sure that there are three floors before you call her later? If it has three floors, do you think it would be fun for Ginna to have her own room downstairs? It would be good for her to have her own space.

Before I forget, could you also ask her about how the place is heated in the winter? I've heard that this old cabin can get very cold. Maybe it has a fire place, that would be romantic. Also, we need to know how far the nearest middle school is, don't forget Ginna finishes elementary school next year.

Best regards,
Amy Forest

**191.** According to the advertisement, which of the following is NOT true about TAYLOR cabin?

(A) It is recently painted.
(B) It is located near the convenient shops.
(C) It has friendly neighbors.
(D) It was bought expensively.

**192.** Who will Mr. Mark Ashley most likely be?

(A) Ms. Lisa Brook's president
(B) A real estate agency
(C) The owner of the cabin
(D) Ginna's father

**193.** Which of the following doesn't Ms. Lisa Brook ask Mr. Mark Ashley?

(A) To ask if there is a middle school
(B) To check how to operate the heating system in winter
(C) To have enough parking space
(D) To inquire how many floors TAYLOR cabin has

**194.** In the e-mail, the word "romantic", line 3, paragraph 3, is closest in meaning to?

(A) sentimental
(B) practical
(C) interesting
(D) fantastic

**195.** What will Mr. Mark Ashley do next?

(A) Contact Ms. Lisa Brook in the evening
(B) Wait for Ms. Lisa Brook's call
(C) Search for a middle school
(D) Expect the sale of his cabin

*GO ON TO THE NEXT PAGE*

---

**NOTICE**

If you lost your luggage, it will be compensated for with a daily allowance of up to $100 per each item until it is found. Otherwise $3,500 per lost item will be paid.

If you experience any difficulties during your trip with JetBlue Air, please contact the support service using the web-site at jetblue.net.

Luggage ID : HCT923904
Flight : #DQ845
Departing from : Chicago/US
Landing in : London/UK

---

To : Shion Cooper <shion111@gmail.com>
From : Todd Hamilton <toddh@jetblue.net>
Date : October 13
Sub : Re : Luggage

Dear Ms. Shion Cooper,

I am happy to notify you that finally we have found your luggage (Luggage ID : HCT923904). The ground staff had accidentlly mislabelled your luggage, and it was sent to Paris instead of the original destination. We have calculated that you have been missing your luggage for a total 30 days and have made a payment of $3,000 to your bank account according to the luggage notice and the confirmation e-mail you received immediately after reserving your ticket.

Please, let me know where you would like to have your suitcase sent. However, you should keep in mind that we are limited to destinations that JetBlue air flies to.

Sincerely

Todd Hamilton
Client Service Director, JetBlue Air

| To | Todd Hamilton <toddh@jetblue.net> |
| --- | --- |
| From | Shion Cooper <shion111@gmail.com> |
| Date | October 13 |
| Subject | Re : Re> Luggage |

Dear Mr. Todd Hamilton

I want to thank you for sending the e-mail regarding my lost luggage. Without one of my suitcases, I spent about a month in London. I will be in Brighton, England for a few months and I have already replaced most of the things that were missing. If I pay for shipping, could you have my suitcase delivered from Chicago Airport to my hometown of Port Clinton? I am sure you still have my address details in your system.

Best regards,
Shion Cooper

196. According to the notice, how is Ms. Shion Cooper instructed to contact Jetblue Air?

(A) By ringing the service desk
(B) By visiting JetBlue air's homepage
(C) By sending her e-mail
(D) By going to the airport office in person

197. Why does Mr. Todd Hamilton send his e-mail to Ms. Shion Cooper?

(A) To inform her that she can take steps
(B) To apologize for an expensive ticket
(C) To notify her of the location of her suitcase
(D) To ask her to check her belongings

198. What can be inferred about Ms. Shion Cooper?

(A) She lost a piece of luggage.
(B) She worked at Jetblue Air before.
(C) She is missing her passport at Chicago airport.
(D) She has already met Mr. Todd Hamilton.

199. Why was Ms. Shion Cooper's luggage sent to Paris?

(A) Because Mr. Hamilton didn't know where Ms. Cooper would like to have her suitcase sent
(B) Because JetBlue Air can't calculate that Ms. Cooper will have been without her luggage for a total 30 days
(C) Because An employee of JetBlue Air applied the wrong tag to Ms. Cooper's suitcase
(D) Because Mr. Hamilton didn't know that JetBlue Air is limited destinations

200. Where does Ms. Cooper want to send her luggage?

(A) Chicago
(B) London
(C) Brighton
(D) Port Clinton

**Stop! This is the end of the test. If you finish before time is called, you may go back to Parts 5, 6, and 7 and check your work.**

*GO ON TO THE NEXT PAGE*

퀵 토익 실전모의고사 SET #3 정답

| | 응시일 | TEST 소요시간 | 맞은 개수 | 환산 점수 |
|---|---|---|---|---|
| LC | ___월___일 | _____분 | _____개 | _____점 |
| RC | | _____분 | _____개 | _____점 |

| PART 1 | PART 2 | PART 3 | | PART 4 | PART 5 | PART 6 | PART 7 | | |
|---|---|---|---|---|---|---|---|---|---|
| 1 (C) | 7 (B) | 32 (D) | 62 (A) | 71 (C) | 101 (D) | 131 (D) | 147 (B) | 176 (D) | 186 (D) |
| 2 (A) | 8 (C) | 33 (B) | 63 (D) | 72 (A) | 102 (C) | 132 (A) | 148 (D) | 177 (C) | 187 (D) |
| 3 (B) | 9 (A) | 34 (A) | 64 (D) | 73 (D) | 103 (C) | 133 (B) | 149 (C) | 178 (B) | 188 (A) |
| 4 (B) | 10 (A) | 35 (D) | 65 (B) | 74 (D) | 104 (D) | 134 (B) | 150 (D) | 179 (A) | 189 (C) |
| 5 (A) | 11 (C) | 36 (D) | 66 (B) | 75 (C) | 105 (D) | 135 (C) | 151 (B) | 180 (D) | 190 (C) |
| 6 (D) | 12 (A) | 37 (B) | 67 (D) | 76 (B) | 106 (C) | 136 (C) | 152 (D) | 181 (B) | 191 (D) |
| | 13 (C) | 38 (D) | 68 (D) | 77 (C) | 107 (A) | 137 (D) | 153 (B) | 182 (C) | 192 (C) |
| | 14 (B) | 39 (C) | 69 (B) | 78 (A) | 108 (B) | 138 (A) | 154 (C) | 183 (B) | 193 (D) |
| | 15 (C) | 40 (B) | 70 (D) | 79 (B) | 109 (B) | 139 (A) | 155 (B) | 184 (A) | 194 (A) |
| | 16 (A) | 41 (D) | | 80 (D) | 110 (D) | 140 (C) | 156 (B) | 185 (A) | 195 (A) |
| | 17 (C) | 42 (B) | | 81 (D) | 111 (D) | 141 (D) | 157 (B) | | 196 (B) |
| | 18 (C) | 43 (D) | | 82 (B) | 112 (C) | 142 (B) | 158 (D) | | 197 (C) |
| | 19 (B) | 44 (C) | | 83 (A) | 113 (B) | 143 (C) | 159 (D) | | 198 (A) |
| | 20 (C) | 45 (C) | | 84 (C) | 114 (D) | 144 (B) | 160 (C) | | 199 (C) |
| | 21 (B) | 46 (B) | | 85 (C) | 115 (C) | 145 (D) | 161 (C) | | 200 (D) |
| | 22 (C) | 47 (C) | | 86 (C) | 116 (D) | 146 (A) | 162 (D) | | |
| | 23 (A) | 48 (A) | | 87 (D) | 117 (C) | | 163 (B) | | |
| | 24 (C) | 49 (C) | | 88 (B) | 118 (D) | | 164 (C) | | |
| | 25 (B) | 50 (C) | | 89 (D) | 119 (A) | | 165 (D) | | |
| | 26 (C) | 51 (A) | | 90 (C) | 120 (D) | | 166 (A) | | |
| | 27 (C) | 52 (A) | | 91 (C) | 121 (D) | | 167 (B) | | |
| | 28 (B) | 53 (D) | | 92 (B) | 122 (D) | | 168 (C) | | |
| | 29 (A) | 54 (A) | | 93 (D) | 123 (A) | | 169 (B) | | |
| | 30 (B) | 55 (C) | | 94 (B) | 124 (B) | | 170 (B) | | |
| | 31 (A) | 56 (C) | | 95 (D) | 125 (B) | | 171 (C) | | |
| | | 57 (C) | | 96 (A) | 126 (C) | | 172 (B) | | |
| | | 58 (D) | | 97 (B) | 127 (C) | | 173 (C) | | |
| | | 59 (A) | | 98 (A) | 128 (C) | | 174 (B) | | |
| | | 60 (D) | | 99 (A) | 129 (D) | | 175 (D) | | |
| | | 61 (A) | | 100 (D) | 130 (C) | | | | |